To ~~Nerea~~,

my great friend!

Deane C. Eastman

Refining Fire

New Healing
for
Old Wounds

Duane C. Eastman

WESTBOW
PRESS®
A DIVISION OF THOMAS NELSON
& ZONDERVAN

Scripture quotations are taken from the Holy Bible, New International Version®, NIV®. Copyright © 1973, 1978, 1984, 2011 by Biblica, Inc.™ Used by permission of Zondervan. All rights reserved worldwide.

WestBow Press books may be ordered through booksellers or by contacting:

WestBow Press
A Division of Thomas Nelson & Zondervan
1663 Liberty Drive
Bloomington, IN 47403
www.westbowpress.com
1 (866) 928-1240

ISBN: 978-1-5127-7666-9 (sc)
ISBN: 978-1-5127-7667-6 (hc)
ISBN: 978-1-5127-7665-2 (e)

Library of Congress Control Number: 2017902932

Print information available on the last page.

WestBow Press rev. date: 3/3/2017

To the churches I was called to shepherd:

- ❖ Bethel Evangelical Methodist Church, Ridgefield, WA (Pastor)
- ❖ First Baptist Church, Portland, OR (Associate Pastor)
- ❖ First Baptist Church, Athena, OR (Pastor)
- ❖ Judson Baptist Church, Salem, OR (Pastor)
- ❖ First Baptist Church, Anacortes, WA (Pastor)
- ❖ First Baptist Church, Lamar, CO (Interim Pastor)
- ❖ First Baptist Church, Ontario, OR (Interim Pastor)
- ❖ First Baptist Church, Kent, WA (Interim Pastor)
- ❖ New Baptist Church, Huntington, WV (Associate Pastor)

To him be glory in the church and in Christ Jesus throughout all generations, for ever and ever! Amen.

—Ephesians 3:21

Contents

Introduction

This is a book for healing wounded churches. When a church experiences conflict, the result is a fellowship of wounded people. Therefore, this is also for healing wounded souls. Healing for the church involves a healing of the people involved. The process of healing is essentially the same for both. That is because the church is God's vessel for healing the deep wounds of the human soul. Conversely, the relational, emotional, and spiritual recovery of individuals is the key for a local congregation to experience renewal and fulfill her mission. A church and its people are one and the same.

Conflict and division has been the experience of the church ever since Paul and Barnabas argued over John Mark and went their separate ways (Acts 15:39). More often than not, divisions occur over people. Even theological debates end up as battles between individuals or groups of people. That's because individuals identify with positions, doctrines, and the mundane issues of the church, often making the mistake of allowing a person or an issue to become more important than the unity of the fellowship. Like the fire that destroyed the temple in Jerusalem, conflict seems to be consuming the church these days, reducing God's vessel of redemption and hope to a smoldering rubble. But fire can also be a purifying, healing agent. It is the way of God, through the power of His Spirit, to transform the destructive fires of conflict into a refining blaze of healing so that what emerges is a church in the true image of Jesus Christ.

The healing process set forth in this book is the application of biblical principles of grace that actually work. They have been tested and found to be amazingly effective. Damaged churches *can* experience renewal and become effective vessels of healing grace to their community. Wounded believers *can* experience renewal and restoration, discovering a dimension of God's presence either forgotten or never before known.

Understanding the reasons for conflict and division, rediscovering the healing impact of Jesus's mission, catching a new vision of what it means to be the church in today's world, and designing a local fellowship so that a healing grace defines worship and ministry is the focus of this book. As such, it is both a manual for personal healing of the deep wounds of the soul and for healing the wounded church.

Part I

The Need for Healing

CHAPTER 1

Fire

> These have come so that your faith—of greater worth
> than gold, which perishes even though refined by
> fire—may be proved genuine and may result in praise,
> glory and honor when Jesus Christ is revealed.
> —1 Peter 1:7

When I was six years old, our country home was consumed by fire. It was a Saturday afternoon. My father and two older brothers were at the cattle auction. My mother and baby brother were at a community gathering, and I was with two older sisters and a cousin at the Saturday afternoon matinee in town. When we returned home, all that was left of our house was a basement full of ashes. That fire was a change agent with many consequences for my family, not the least of which was to inspire my parents to return to church. Like many couples, they had become consumed by the needs and activities of work and family, which relegated faith and church to an occasional moment on special days. The fire was a real wake-up call. Shortly thereafter, with their brood in tow, they sought out a local congregation and became committed members. Thus began my journey with the church. Over the next dozen years, that local community of believers introduced me to Jesus Christ as my Savior, connected music to my sense of worship, and anchored me in the Word of God as the basis for life and faith. Unfortunately, they also introduced me to the frequent ritual of congregational conflict.

It was after I graduated from high school and had moved to Oregon to work as a logger that my home church, once a growing, joyful congregation, experienced division and decline, eventually closing its doors. Looking back over a lifetime of pastoral ministry, I now know that the seeds of conflict were evident in that church long before division did its destructive work. The outright breakdown of relationships was merely a symptom of division that had been taking place over a long period of time, like a fire that smolders long and furtively before erupting into open flame. How it happens in a church is much the same as it does in marriages, partnerships, and friendships. Criticism replaces compassion. Minor irritations become major issues. Personalities, preferences, and perceptions become elevated above love, understanding, and patience.

Sunday dinners were always special. We were either at someone else's home after church or had guests at ours. While it did not mean anything to an adolescent boy who was more interested in getting a drumstick off the plate of fried chicken or a sizable piece of elk roast, the growing critical conversations turned the feast after worship into a buffet of spiritual poison. At first, they dissected the bishop, along with denominational decisions and policies, rarely with any positive conclusions. That spirit of complaint soon infected members of the congregation in how they approached one another. The pastor, a godly servant, fell under criticism as some members found fault in one thing after another. Unhappy people always blame others for their misery. It is spiritual dysfunction, a weed of complaint and dissatisfaction growing in the complainer's heart, choking out the wheat of love and trust. In contrast, people who walk in the Holy Spirit nurture love, trust, and grace and in so doing discover the secret of "being content whatever the circumstances … in any and every situation" (Philippians 4:11–12). Criticism, complaining, negative comments, gossip, slander, and being judgmental of others are the ways of the Pharisee. They reflect the very opposite of Jesus's mandates to love, extend the grace of compassion and understanding, and embrace lifestyles that serve others. Critical and judging attitudes and activities are the primary tools used by the enemy of God to thwart the divine purpose.

A negative, judging spirit is the bane of the church, much more deadly to the way than any atheistic philosophy or humanistic value decreed as normal by the high court. They are attitudes that always emit from self-centered, pride-filled hearts that attempt to exercise control and power over others . From the beginning it has been the primary form of temptation used by the serpent, beginning with Eve and Adam, to put into the human mind a subtle criticism of God: "Did God really say?" (Genesis 3:1). It was a thinly veiled suggestion that God's motives and methods are suspect. Ultimately, our criticism of others in the church is criticism of God, and passing judgment on others usurps the place of God. To treat others as unworthy and reject them is to render Christ's atonement as unworthy and a rejection of him. It is to deny the sovereignty of God in favor of our own sense of purpose and self-satisfaction.

J. I. Packer, in his book *A Passion for Faithfulness*, points out that the name of *devil* is really a "descriptive title which means 'slanderer,' one who thinks, speaks and plans evil, first against God himself, secondly against the human race. His name in Hebrew is 'Abaddon,' and in Greek, Apollyon' (Revelation 9:11)—both names meaning 'destroyer.' For his fierce sustained, pitiless hatred of humanity Satan is spoken of as a murderer, the evil one, a roaring and devouring lion, and a great red dragon. For his habit of twisting truth as a means to his ends he is called a liar and deceiver. He is malicious, mean, ugly, and cruel to the last degree. ... he is extremely cunning, much cleverer than we are and is highly skilled at manipulating and using people to bring about his destructive goals."[1]

Because the church is the unique vessel ordained by God to fulfill His plan of redemption, Apollyon's most effective tool is to destroy the unity of the fellowship by breaking the bond of peace (Ephesians 4:3) using conflict and division. To do that he needs inside help, professors of faith who become terrorists of the truth and church leadership who operate with power and control by sowing seeds of division among the fellowship (Matthew 13:25). It is no surprise that Jesus listed *slander, false testimony, evil thoughts, malice, envy,* and *arrogance* alongside *murder, adultery, sexual immorality, theft, greed, deceit,* and *lewdness* as the great spiritual evils (Matthew 15:19, Mark 7:22). They are evil for many reasons, ultimately because they are the common weapons used by the enemy to destroy the church.

Paul echoed the awareness that the most deadly threat to the church is the presence of these destructive activities. He wrote to the church at Corinth, "I fear that there may be quarreling, jealousy, outbursts of anger, factions, slander, gossip, arrogance and disorder" (2 Corinthians 12:20); to the church at Ephesus, "Get rid of all bitterness, rage and anger, brawling and slander, along with every form of malice" (Ephesians 4:31); to the church at Colosse, "But now you must rid yourselves of all such things as these: anger, rage, malice, slander, and filthy language from your lips" (Colossians 3:8).

James admonished the early church, "Brothers, do not slander one another. Anyone who speaks against his brother or judges him speaks against the law and judges it. When you judge the law, you are not keeping it, but sitting in judgment on it" (James 4:11). Likewise, Peter wrote to the believers scattered by

---

[1] J. I. Packer, *A Passion for Faithfulness* (Wheaton, Illinois: Crossways, 1995), 94.

cruel persecution to "rid yourselves of all malice and all deceit, hypocrisy, envy, and slander of every kind" (1 Peter 2:1).

It seems that the chaos of congregations is in direct proportion to the presence of those activities and attitudes. Conversely, the presence of the Spirit is expressed in unity and love, and it results in a congregation that is an effective vessel of grace to wounded and broken souls. There is an either/or factor at work. The level of prayer, compassion, love, grace, and an attitude of serving by a congregation is in direct proportion to the absence of gossip, criticism, judging, and a power/control relationship. The presence of the Holy Spirit is evidenced by the aroma of unity and peace, and His absence is evidenced by the stench of self-seeking and conflict.

My first pastor was eventually pressured into resigning. Because his youngest son was a friend of mine, I was often in their home and witnessed some of the pain and anguish of that faithful servant. It would be later in my own angst of ministry that I would understand what he was experiencing. He resigned and an exciting younger couple, who had been professional musicians, were called as pastors to lead the congregation to the promised land. They were there during my adolescent years, and for me they filled many of those important needs of a teenager for spiritual mentorship. They were musically gifted and their music soothed the beast at first, because it satisfied the personal desires of many members. He was not theologically trained but loved the Lord, and his friendly, charismatic style of ministry served him well.

But the roots of criticism and slander are not easily eradicated, and in time that young pastor, too, fell under the critical scrutiny of unhappy critics. Worship style and interesting sermons are never enough to fix what is wrong. It takes the Spirit moving others to confession and repentance, resulting in transformation of vision, motive, and method so that grace, not gripes, rule the fellowship. They were eventually "starved" out of the ministry and shortly after were divorced, raising many questions in my young idealistic mind: Did their many good works count? Were the many people who had been converted and baptized under their ministry truly saved? And how about the motive and manner of the church—was that congregation of God? I now know something of the pressures ministry places on a servant's marriage and family, and I am sorry that there weren't resources in those days to heal those gifted servants from the pains of marital disaster and rescue them from the clergy's discard pile.

Another pastor was called to serve that wounded, conflicted congregation. He was a good man, a survivor and a committed servant of Christ. But the weeds and thorns of criticism and complaint had grown up and dominated the mood and mentality of the church. What was once healthy debate would inevitably become deadly gossip and accusation. Seeking God's will in prayer and worship gave way to issue-driven reactions. Fear replaced faith, anger and criticism shut out grace and forgiveness, and power and control overwhelmed loving and serving.

I wept. I remember falling a large ponderosa pine tree in the Blue Mountains of Oregon, reflecting on what had transpired in my home church, and then standing on that stump and weeping. Thankfully none of my fellow tough-guy loggers saw my tears. I felt betrayal, confusion, anger, and grief all at the same time. It would not be the last time I would weep over a dysfunctional and disintegrating church. The surprising thing is that my connection to Christ did not diminish. The faithfulness and patience of God is never ending. His ways are beyond our comprehension, but His purposes and plan are just and perfect. How slow we are to understand that eternal fact. I made the critical error of thinking I could serve Jesus apart from involvement in the church. It was a mistake I would repeat more than once in my journey, even leading me to step out of pastoral ministry on a couple of occasions. But every time I came to that faulty conclusion, the Spirit would overhaul my soul, challenging my values and priorities, and ultimately would alter my perceptions of the church.

Eventually I would grow to understand that the church, best exemplified in local congregations, is the living presence of Jesus on earth, *the* vessel in which eternal God vested His redemptive plan. Growing up in evangelicalism, I had learned the official doctrine early on that Jesus came to earth to save *me* by dying on the cross for *my* sin, and that *my* security and hope is sealed by His resurrection from the grave. While it is true that "when He was on the cross, I was on His mind," as the songwriter puts it, such thinking is a limited, privatized, self-centered understanding of God's plan of redemption. It fits our Western, egocentric, individualistic paradigm in which we boil everything down to the question "what does it do for me?" Unfortunately, we have elevated that egocentric version of the gospel in the church to the point that *my* needs are perceived as the primary issue of Sunday worship, the pastoral activity, and even of eternity. As a result, many churches are not communities of servant believers, but gatherings of self-focused individuals who evaluate everything from curb appeal, style of music, order of worship, and especially the sermon, according to their personal expectations, needs, and wants. While it is wonderfully and amazingly true that Jesus came to save *me*, to heal me, and to bless my life, His greater mission was to establish His *church*, not as a collection of individuals, but as a living body doing His work, a unique fellowship designed to be His vessel of grace that becomes His healing touch to a broken world.

"Church conflict" is an oxymoron and a blasphemy. The word *church* reflects healing, grace, forgiveness, love, hope, inclusion, welcome, recovery, renewal, transformation, and other positive, Christ-like values, all of which are the very antithesis of conflict and division. Unfortunately, for many people, the very word "church" elicits feelings of anger, conflict, rejection, wounding, prejudice, pain, judging, condemnation, and other negative connotations. Conflict seems to be the norm for many congregations. If we look for a wounded, broken, conflicted church, we usually don't have to look very far, often not even beyond our own foyer. How Jesus must weep! His prayer in the Garden of Gesthamene was a plea for His followers (the church!) to live in unity (not to be confused with uniformity) so that the world would come to know the Father. We, the church, are ordained by God as the unique vessel, empowered by His Spirit, to be His agency of grace, a living, visible presence of God in the world. Unity in the church validates the message of forgiveness, love and hope, a message and reality desperately needed in our world of terror and conflict. "Church," as Jesus intended, ultimately means peace, refuge, and safety. Some of His final words reflect that meaning: "Peace I leave with you; my peace I give you. I do not give to you as the world gives. Do not let your hearts be troubled and do not be afraid" (John 14:27). Sadly, in the two thousand years of Christian history, instead of unity His church at all levels is often rendered impotent with conflict.

One of the most tragic accounts I can imagine is that of someone desperate for meaning, healing, and hope, a soul damaged and wounded by the issues of life, who finally walks through the door of a church building in search of God. But instead of experiencing a community of love, grace, and acceptance by a congregation of redeemed sinners who extend to others God's redemptive grace, they are subjected to terrorists of the soul who inflict condemnation, criticism, and rejection and who practice exclusion. Add to that the fact that too often a seeker discovers a congregation in some kind of power struggle with open conflict. The result is that the very vessel ordained of God to heal people does the opposite. Instead of being the place of peace, a fellowship of wounded healers, conflicted churches are wounding hurters. The question is haunting: If the church of Jesus Christ fails to be a vessel of grace and healing, where else can desperate souls go to find hope? Will they be redeemed by the government, our judicial courts, the halls of higher education, or Hollywood? There is only one ordained vessel of grace, one unique image bearer of the Redeemer, one agency ordained by God to be the living body of Christ in the world. It is the church, best expressed in local congregations.

I would be happy if readers could dismiss the above scenario as an aberration and prove that most churches today are refuges of peace where grace and love rule without conflict. Unfortunately, it seems that such congregations of grace and peace are exceptions instead of the norm. This raises some troubling questions. Why do so many churches get embroiled in conflict and become divided? What has gone wrong? How can wounded, broken, and divided churches experience healing and renewal so that they can become God's vessel of healing and hope to the community around them? There are many solutions proposed these days to fix the declining church. The most popular have to do with changing worship style, ministry emphasis, and personalities, all important issues to consider. But I would contend that the problem isn't that easily fixed. The reason being that the real problem is systemic, a dysfunction at the core, an issue of the root upon which we base our perceptions, meanings, purposes and actions.

Not all churches are in conflict. There are many wonderful fellowships of grace. They are modern *cities of refuge* where people of any kind, condition, or need can enter in and experience the healing presence of God. They are sanctuaries of love and grace, oases to the soul in the desert of hedonistic values, training centers where disciples develop understanding of truth in the confusion of postmodernity, hospitals of the heart where the balm of Gilead is applied with genuine compassion.

Likewise, few of the people in conflicted, divided, broken, and wounded churches are evil. In fact, the very activities that lead to ecclesial chaos are often the desperate actions of people wanting change and renewal. They are wrong and destructive because they emerge out of personal agendas, wrong assumptions, or established traditions that, when involving power, control, anger, slander, gossip, and other self-centered behaviors, are never healing but always destructive.

The good news is that wounded, dysfunctional, broken congregations can experience healing, spiritual transformation and renewal. It is God's will that His people overcome difficult circumstances and escape from the painful past, becoming effective vessels of grace. The Spirit of God is a fire that doesn't just destroy—it refines and heals the wounded and broken congregations so that they "may be proved genuine and may result in praise, glory and honor when Jesus Christ is revealed" (1 Peter 1:7). It is never a quick fix, nor is it as simple as invoking a new program, starting a new ministry, changing worship styles, or hiring new professional leaders. While any or all of those "fixes" may or may not be necessary, the secret to healing and renewal occurs at a much deeper level, are more difficult, and ultimately involve something that we cannot do *for, of,* or *by* ourselves.

CHAPTER 2

The Call

I press on to take hold of that for which Christ Jesus took hold of me.
—Philippians 3:12

Does God call specific individuals to pastoral ministry? If so, what does that call look like? How does a man or woman who is devoted to Christ hear the call of God to serve? The answers are important, for without a divinely ordained shepherd, a local congregation will be compromised by alternative agendas and will lack spiritual discernment. Paul realized that "the call" is to be sold out to a life of being God's agent of grace. It is to be in the grasp of Jesus Christ and to pursue the same agenda He exercised. The critical essential role of a godly pastoral leader cannot be understated. It is therefore important that both the pastor and the people of a congregation are aware that the pastor is called and ordained by God.

My personal journey to understanding my call to ministry took a long and irregular path. When I was twelve years old, I accepted Christ as my Savior during evangelistic meetings held in my church. Although I was an innocent, naïve, twelve-year-old farm boy, the conviction of the Spirit was powerful on me, and I had a genuine and emotional conversion experience. From that moment forward, I never doubted God's hand on my life. But it would be many years before I would understand and fully respond to His call. I had to learn some painful but necessary lessons. I now know a childhood conversion does not automatically translate into an obedient life.

The people in my church began talking about my going into the ministry. It was not something I had said, and I was uncomfortable with the presupposition being made. There was provision in the denomination's discipline manual for a "quarterly conference preacher," a way of introducing young people into the ministry. After meeting with the bishop and the pastor (an event I vaguely remember), I received a license to preach and was expected to do so at my home church at least once a year. That "call" to preach was supported by the local Youth For Christ program. They sponsored an annual "preacher" contest in which aspiring teenage preachers would give a sermon at a youth convention in the form of a competitive event. I was coerced to enter the contest, and then I was declared the winner. For me it felt rigged as another attempt to force me into a role I wasn't sure I wanted. I was feeling manipulated and literally shoved toward the ministry. My reaction was to resent and resist the attempt of others to control my life. By the time I was a senior in high school, I would arrive at church late and leave during the benediction so no one would corner me with their offers to help me to go to college in preparation for the ministry. On one occasion I was handed a considerable sum of money, more than I had ever seen at one time, on the condition of what college to attend. Again I felt manipulated, and I angrily rejected it. Soon thereafter at the age of nineteen, I headed to Oregon to fall timber.

God has been called the "hound of heaven." He pursues us in ways we can never imagine. As the Psalmist cries out, "If I go up to the heavens, you are there; if I make my bed in the depths, you are there. If I rise on the wings of the dawn, if I settle on the far side of the sea, even there your hand will guide me, your right hand will hold me fast. If I say, "Surely the darkness will hide me and the light become night around me," even the darkness will not be dark to you; the night will shine like the day, for darkness is as light to you" (Ps. 139:8–12). Realizing in my heart that I was trying to run from God, my life in Oregon consisted of working weekdays, hunting and fishing on weekends, and attending different churches when I felt like it. However, God's call was constantly echoing in my mind. That fact was evident in a series of events that resulted in my going to Bible college.

Working in the woods is risky, and one has to be careful and constantly live with a certain sense of danger. One day I was standing on a small pile of large logs when they shifted and rolled. When things stopped moving, my left leg was trapped between two large logs, each weighing close to a ton. The pain was excruciating, and I was aware that if they rolled again, I would be crushed to death. The only other person around was an equipment operator, a small man who had only one good leg. He hobbled the thirty feet to the small end of the log where he could get his arms around it and, with superhuman strength, lift it up until I could pull my leg out. It was a miracle of biblical proportions, an utter impossibility for him to do that.

The next day I couldn't stand on my black-and-blue leg. Amazingly, no one told me to see a doctor! The boss came to my door and said to me, "You can't stay at home all day. Maybe you can't fall trees, but you can drive the wide-load pickup truck while I move the log loader from one canyon to another." So I drove an old pickup truck loaded with fuel cans, driving ahead of a large log loader, up one canyon, across beautiful mountain meadows, and down into another canyon. When I started down the steep, narrow road into the other canyon, I applied the brakes, only to realize the brake pedal went to the floor. As my speed increased, I shifted into a lower gear, but to no avail. At an opportune moment, on a sharp switchback turn, I drove up the bank until the pickup's momentum stopped, and then I hung on as it rolled down the hillside to the road below. One more roll and I would have rolled off a sheer cliff to certain death.

This time I was sent to the doctor and emerged with bruises and cuts, but no serious damage. In reflecting on the recent incidences, I thought it was just a series of unfortunate happenings, so I never gave it much theological thought. But such events continued to take place. A couple of weeks later, I was falling a large snag (dead tree) on a very steep hillside. In an unusual twist, instead of the top of the tree tipping down the slope, it jumped off the stump right at me. I ran as fast as I could down the mountainside, with the tree digging holes in the ground right on my heels. Finally, I was able to move to one side and allow it to slide on past. I was so frightened that my "hand went limp and my knees became as weak as water" (Ezekiel 7:17). It took several minutes before I had enough strength to climb back up the hill and retrieve my power saw.

The final incident took place a few days later. I felled an exceptionally large pine tree and, as the custom was, when the gap of the saw-cut began to increase, I yelled, "Timber!" to alert everyone in the area a tree was coming down. Stepping back, I looked at the target spot for the tree to fall, and to my horror there stood my falling partner. He was running his chainsaw and not able to hear my shout. It was one of those slow-moving, nightmare scenes. I screamed and waved my arms, but he was facing away from me. The huge tree gathered momentum as gravity pulled it down to the ground. It hit with a loud crash, and dust boiled up blocking my view. I was sure I had killed a man. When the dust cleared away, he stood there, only inches from the very tip of that giant tree, looking at me as if to say, "No big deal." Then I did want to kill him, for he never should have been there in the first place, and at twenty years of age, he had caused me to almost have a heart attack.

The next day I quit my job, loaded my belongings into my car, and headed for Bible college. There I studied the Bible, was immersed in church doctrine, and met the woman who would become my lifelong partner in life and in ministry. After three years I was graduated, and we were married and headed out to find what the Lord had in store for us. There was, however, still much to learn.

In my early years of ministry I anticipated a life of preaching to a large congregation of nice spiritual people in a comfortable church. Perhaps typical of beginning pastors, it was a fantasy rooted in my immature and uninformed assumptions. In time I would learn that more important than the size or location of the congregation would be for me to surrender to God's purposes for my life. For all believers, regardless of occupation or calling, the most important and consistent issue is to accept God's will rather than pursue my own agendas. True success is not found in the fulfillment of our own dreams, but in the daily exercise of a heart that finds delight in being obedient to God's will. Personally, my self-aggrandized dream revealed my need to be healed, which would require forgiveness and transformation. God has a habit of using unlikely people for His purposes (using the foolish to confound the wise). Instead of serving in those pastures of peace and tranquility, most of my pastoral ministry has been to heal the wounded, love the conflicted, and serve needy congregations. Without question, God's ways are beyond understanding.

The calling that I was so slow to accept was a gift of God's grace, for it was, first of all, a call to experience personal healing. Further, to witness the miracle of healing and renewal of a wounded congregation—so that fear, anger, mistrust and anxiety are replaced by faith, grace, trust, and confident hope— has profoundly impacted my personal journey of faith. God has always been in the business of redemption, restoration, and renewal. Beyond any shadow of doubt, He stands ready to transform and renew all who turn to Him and cry out for healing. While I have not suffered anything close to that of ancient Job, my spirit responds to his proclamation as he stood in the midst of absolute disaster and announced, "I know my redeemer lives" (Job 19:25).

It is possible for individuals and congregations to overcome the past. In doing so, healing and renewal becomes a reality where love, grace, and compassion rule. I have witnessed the miracle of the resurrection play out in congregations. As a result of the right vision and doing the right things for the right reason, any fellowship of believers can become a place of grace and peace so that badly damaged souls will, through them, experience the miracle of redemption and hope.

While working toward my baccalaureate degree, my first opportunity to pastor was in a small, country church. The church's history had been one of prolonged conflict involving a few strong personalities, one of whom was the pastor. In a debate over what to do with some property they had been gifted, the pastor's vision was one thing, the congregation's another. When the vote went against the pastor's wishes, he left the meeting angry, informing them that he wouldn't be there Sunday. The next day he packed up and left, leaving a broken, confused congregation behind. They contacted me at a time when I needed employment and they needed to fill the pulpit while they searched for another pastor. Soon, they called me to be their pastor. It was mutually beneficial, for they could not afford a "real" pastor, and I was thrilled to have any pulpit from which to preach. However, one thing was certain. I did not know how to deal with a church, even a small one, of conflicted, hurting people. So I did nothing except to love them and do my best to preach the grace of Christ. The congregation began to experience a measure of healing and growth. Ironically, because of my immaturity and idealism about the church, at the same time they began to heal, I began to experience conflict.

It happened at an annual meeting of that church's denomination. I was shocked at the abuse of power and the exercise of unholy politics by denominational leaders. My indignation turned into anger and I decided to reject the "organized" church. I concluded that while I would serve the Lord, it would not be as pastor of a local church. There are too many hypocrites! So

I resigned my pulpit and signed a contract to teach at a large, suburban high school. Little did I know that when it came to political hypocrisy and the use of power and innuendo, I had jumped from the frying pan into the fire! After just two of years of teaching, I was invited to join the staff of a large, inner-city church as an administrative associate. It was an opportunity I could not pass up.

But the refining fire of God was about to get hotter for me as my simplistic view of congregational life was challenged by an exciting and complex church. On the one hand, I was introduced to positive methods of dealing with difficult people and explosive situations. On the other hand, I increasingly became aware of my faults, weaknesses, and failures. Again, I stepped aside from pastoral ministry, only this time instead of doing so because of the fault of others, I was acutely aware of my own challenges to measure up to the demands of my calling.

For a year I worked at a secular job while processing through my own failures and inadequacies. Finally, in a spiritual epiphany, twenty-five years after my conversion experience I came to fully accept God's call on my life.

Soon I received a call to serve a small-town church in a remote area of Oregon. They were struggling with the sudden exit of their previous pastor, who had acted on an immoral impulse. In accepting the call to be their pastor, we became a wounded congregation and a wounded pastor who together would experience God's healing grace. It was in that setting that I fully recognized God's call and plan for my life, which was to be a servant leader of grace in a local church. In the process, I began to discover the church Jesus established, which is different from the kind I had envisioned and experienced before. Jesus called it His *ekklesia,* a Greek word that means "a called-out community." He obviously did not have in mind a gathering of people who used religion to exercise political power. Instead it is a mystical community of people who are objects of Christ's grace while being agents of His grace to others. It was in that remote church in Oregon that the reality of grace began to shape my heart and mind as well as my discovery of the ekklesia. It was a blessed experience of healing and renewal for both pastor and church.

The next call was to a suburban congregation in a city, a fellowship distressed and uncertain as a result of some bizarre behavior of an unhappy pastor. For them it was needed lessons of grace and the discovery of trust in allowing God's sovereign will to be fulfilled. At the same time, renewed theology of the church was emerging in my thinking. In the process of serving wounded congregations, I was discovering that the divine plan *is* about the church. In spite of the faults of her people (maybe because of them), and in spite of the limitations and failures of some pastoral leaders, local congregations provide the environment for the Holy Spirit to apply the powerful grace of Christ Jesus to people's lives. What is important is not that everyone is perfectly holy, but that grace and love become the dominating factors in the life of a congregation. It isn't the size or the wealth or the past history of a congregation that matters. What really counts is that it is a community where Jesus is alive through the surrender of individual wills to the leading of the Holy Spirit. That is the key for healing wounded churches, and it inevitably results in a place where needy, hurting seekers discover Christ.

For the next fourteen years, I served a congregation in an upscale, small town that is transitioning from a fishing and logging economy to an attractive retirement and outdoor-recreation community. This congregation's painful wound ran deep, the result of a long season of conflict that finally erupted into a full-blown church split. A large group of members exited from a congregational meeting and started another church in town. Some families were divided between the two congregations. Many members simply vanished, not wanting to take sides or to experience any more church conflict. The remnant left behind was mostly senior adults, devastated and small in number, about a third of the previous congregation. Once again the message of grace and ministries of love, seasoned with many prayers, brought healing to the wound members as the church community experienced restoration to a whole and holy mission.

All the churches with which I have been associated have godly people in them. I cherish deeply the relationships and the experiences gained. Every one of the above churches experienced the healing power of applied grace. They are fellowships where the Spirit of God empowers them to be His agency of healing and transformation to people in their community.

Along the way something happened to my conditional relationship to the church. I am convinced that the ekklesia is the best thing to hit human history since the surgery on Adam that resulted in Eve. Of course, I am talking about the church as preordained by God, established by Christ, and empowered by the Holy Spirit. As such it is often radically different from the many alternative versions that claim the title of "church" but are not temples of grace. Reclaiming the church through spiritual renewal is a critical agenda for today's believers. It will require some "called" servant pastors and some major healing activities.

The apostle Paul used what had happened in the churches he served to validate his call and ministry. In the same way, I look at the congregations I served and see the healed fellowships and devotion to Christ's kingdom that developed. That is validation of God's call. It is a poignant reminder of the critical importance that the servant pastor is called by God and ordained by the Holy Spirit. When that happens, the agenda is about proclaiming God's grace while preparing people for the work of ministry (Ephesians 4:12). No other agenda will suffice.

Following are some of my observations, experiences, and perceptions as to what brings healing to a wounded congregation. It is not intended to be comprehensive, but merely a sharing of what I have discovered and experienced through the grace of God. I love the church. My passion in life and ministry is for Christ's church. While the church of Jesus Christ is universal and diverse, I believe it is best expressed and fulfilled in the grace-filled ministry of local fellowships where people of all kinds and experiences are called to Christ, healed, nurtured to become Jesus's disciples, and empowered to be effective kingdom servants. I believe that the renewal and restoration of local churches is *the* critical issue facing us today. I also believe that the confusion brought to the table by twenty-first-century postmodernity is best answered by Spirit-filled, grace-defined, love-motivated local congregations. That is as God planned!

In the chapters that follow is a Bible-based theology of the church as the ultimate, unique, and universal expression of God's plan of continued redemption. The ineffective nature of many church functions, the compromise by congregations to the ways and means of the world, and the often high level of dysfunction, division, and distortion in the church reveals the critical need for a renewed vision of the incredible, invincible, and inspired ekklesia. The following theology of the church will touch on the important systemic issues that format Christ's ekklesia, a biblical review of the principles and practices that empower grace and love to be the identifying and dominant nature of the community, and some suggested paradigms for structuring local churches for ministries of grace.

Chapter 3

Messiah

We have found the Messiah.
—John 1:41

There is a story about a monastery that had once been a great order but had fallen upon hard times. It had dwindled to an abbot and four other monks, all over seventy years old, left in the decaying motherhouse. In the deep woods surrounding the monastery, there was a little hut that a rabbi from a nearby town occasionally used for a hermitage. As he agonized over the imminent death of his order, it occurred to the abbot to visit the hermitage and ask the rabbi if by some possible chance, he could offer any advice that might save the monastery. The rabbi welcomed the abbot at his hut but could only commiserate with him when the abbot explained the purpose of his visit, agreeing that the Spirit had gone out of the people. So the old abbot and the old rabbi wept together, read from the scriptures, and quietly spoke of deep spiritual things. When the abbot had to leave, they embraced each other and agreed that it been wonderful that they had finally met. The abbot said, "But I have still failed in my purpose for coming here. Is there nothing you can tell me, no piece of advice you can give me that would help me save my dying order?"

"No, I am sorry," the rabbi responded. "I have no advice to

give. The only thing I can tell you is that the Messiah is one of you."

When the abbot returned to the monastery, his fellow monks gathered around him to ask, "Well, what did the rabbi say?"

"He couldn't help," the abbot answered. "We just wept and read the scriptures together. The only thing he did say, just as I was leaving, was that the Messiah is one of us. I don't know what he meant."

The old monks wondered if there was any possible significance to the idea that the Messiah was one of them. If so, which one? They begin to see each other through eyes of grace, instead of criticism, and as a result began to treat one another differently on the off chance that one among them might be the Messiah.

Because the forest in which it was situated was beautiful, it so happened that people occasionally visited the monastery to picnic on its tiny lawn and sometimes go into the dilapidated chapel to meditate. Sensing the new aura of respect that now characterized the five old monks, the visitors began to come back to the monastery more frequently to picnic, play, and pray, bringing their friends to show them this special place. Some of the younger men who came to visit the monastery started to talk more and more with the old monks. After a while, one asked if he could join them. Then another asked. And another. So within a few years the monastery had once again become a thriving order and, thanks to the rabbi's gift, a vibrant center of light and spirituality in the realm.[2]

This story is often told to underline the importance of community. The idea that the Messiah is among you is a reminder of the role of the church in the world. No other agency, organization, or institution is ordained of God to be the living presence of the Messiah. Only the church, the ekklesia, the body

[2] M. Scott Peck, *The Different Drum: Community Making and Peace* (New York: Simon & Schuster, 1987), 13–15.

of Christ, the community of believers, is so divinely ordained. Jesus is the man of peace, the God of redemption who extends unconditional forgiveness and love, the healer of body, mind, and soul, the author of hope. The church is the messianic presence of Christ by being His people of peace, healing,and hope. The level of dysfunction, division, and disaster in many churches today reveals a need to be renewed in understanding that the highest priority for the existence of the church is to be the living presence of Christ. This was God's design and purpose from the beginning.

The incarnation of Jesus Christ was necessary because of the brokenness of creation. The impact of sin is experienced in the wounding of humans with the universal need for healing. The divine design and purpose of the church, as the body of Christ, is to be God's agency of that healing. By being conformed to the image of Christ, we are empowered to fulfill God's predetermined purpose. However, when the church experiences division, instead of being the agency of healing, it becomes an agent of sin, contributing to the wounding of people. Understanding the nature and impact of *hamartia*[3] is essential to fulfilling our purpose. The result of sin is always brokenness.

Jesus defines the theme of the ministry of the church as one of healing. It is a new mandate that requires new forms and organizations, new concepts of worship, and a new basis for relationships. When the body of believers exercises the same kind of love exhibited by the life and death of Christ, they not only experience the personal fulfillment of holiness, but also they become a holy environment for healing. For that to be a reality, it is essential that grace becomes the normal experience in congregational vision and style. Grace is the foundational hermeneutic by which the new mandate is interpreted and

---

[3] While there are many nuances to the usage and meaning of "sin" in the Bible, its most basic is that of *hamartia*, usually interpreted as "missing the mark." See chapter 7.

congregational life is determined. The result is a fellowship of mercy in which there is a primary emphasis on imitating Christ.

In some painful ways, many of today's congregations are like the monastery in the story. They are inverted, declining, bickering, and suffering the convulsions that accompany the loss of vision. Conflict has seemingly been a constant plague of the church. The tendency to focus inward and lose vision is forever before the local congregation. One wonders if there has ever been a period of time in the history of the church, at least in America, when so many congregations are wounded.

Divisions have occurred in the church in the past, usually on a large scale in which numerous congregations would join together and separate from the mother denomination over doctrine or a cause. A prime example is the division that occurred in Baptists over the issue of slavery at the time of the Civil War. Diverse biblical interpretation of social and economic issues resulted in the emergence of three separate groups: the Northern Baptists, who were essentially against slavery and for integrated congregations: Southern Baptists, who were for slavery and, therefore, segregated churches according to color; and National Baptist churches, which were made up of African American members. Slavery was not only a social issue but also one that had obvious spiritual ramifications.

In contrast, the fracturing of the church today is generally occurring in local congregations, both large and small, rather than only in denominations. Many of the issues dividing Christians today are social/political in nature but carry significant biblical context as well. Robert Wuthnow writes that the issues that face the church of the twenty-first century will result in a deeper division than those of the past.[4]

Anacortes, Washington, has a population of 15,778, with fourteen Protestant congregations. Four of those congregations

---

[4] Robert Wuthnow, *The Restructuring of American Religion, Society and Faith* Princeton, 1988

have Sunday attendance exceeding two hundred. In the past twenty years, three of the four have experienced a major controversy resulting in either a congregational split or a migration away of a significant numbers of members. The congregation I served, First Baptist Church, experienced a radical division, resulting in the departure of a large segment of the body. That had taken place before my arrival but continued to impact the fellowship. In some of the other congregations (probably in all of them given the reasons for, and severity of, today's dividing issues) differences within the congregation continue to impact the life of the church, hindering growth at the very least, and threatening to close the doors of some.

The disturbing reality of life in religious America is that most congregants and congregations are deeply wounded. It is a tragedy of incredible proportions, for the church is designed by God as His instrument for bring healing and liberation to a world of wounded, enslaved people. How can a wounded congregation be a lighthouse of healing to a violently fractured world? The truth is it can't, at least not very well. We remain in need of the healing Messiah, the One who liberates, heals, and restores us to wholeness, so that we can be vessels of that same healing power to the victims of darkness in the world. We know that the Savior has already come. Yet it is obvious that something is missing, somehow we have gone astray, gotten lost, or lost sight of the Messiah. Again we need to return to original theology—the account of God's design for healing.

A variety of theologies for the church's ministry emphasis abound today. Each offers its own solution to the dysfunction of our world and of the church. Dominion theology proposes a political solution.[5] The Toronto blessing involved a hilarious remedy and claims to have a whole new revelation.[6] The reformed renewal

---

[5] H. Wayne House and Thomas Ice, *Dominion Theology: Blessing or Curse?* (Portland: Multnomah, 1988), 21–24.

[6] James A. Beverly, "Toronto's Mixed Blessing" *Christianity Today,* September 11, 1995, 22–27.

movement directs the church back to reliance on sacramental liturgy.[7]

The most popular and dominant theology impacting the evangelical church today likely falls under the ever-widening umbrella of the "church-growth" movement. It is more than a knee-jerk reaction to the decline of the church in the post-Christian era. The motivation to enlarge the body of believers is deeply rooted in scripture. The mandate of Jesus recorded in Acts 1:8 is the template for the church's evangelical mission.[8] The prospect of growing in numbers by applying the various programs and innovations of the church-growth movement is often seen as the key to their own healing. Many have fallen victim to the belief that doing adopting programming with media appeal will result in numerical growth, which will in turn bring in added income, which will, it is assumed, result in relief from the stresses of conflict and division.

While the problems that are directly related to insufficient numbers of people and inadequate funds are very real, they are more of a by-product than a cause. Engaging in a healthy church growth program or in stewardship education may well be a logical and necessary step toward wholeness. But such emphasis is not the a priori first step toward healing, because the root cause of decline and conflict is the disappearance of grace. Whatever vision drives a conflicted church, it obviously is not the vision of the true Messiah. When we lose the vision of grace, it is common to turn to an external, rather than internal, search for the solution to heal all our diseases. But the problem of a damaged, dying church is an internal one, a condition of the heart. Before any congregation can be the messianic vessel to its community, it has to become whole and holy itself. Authentic growth is a by-product of a healthy, healing congregation that maintains a careful and

---

[7] Smedes, 172–187.

[8] George W. Peters, *A Theology of Church Growth* (Grand Rapids: Zondervan, 1982), 16–20.

conscious focus on the cross of Christ. To be the living presence of Christ in one's community is to rediscover the theology of healing by experiencing the grace of the crucified and risen Christ, the power of the Holy Spirit, and the true purpose of the church of Jesus Christ.

George Barna writes that one of the key distinctions between churches that are healthy and growing, and those that are stagnant or in decline is the existence, or nonexistence, of true vision for ministry.[9] It is worth noting that he adds the qualification "true" to his statement. "A true vision will be one which will align a congregation's heart, mind and actions with God's desires and intentions for ministry."[10] Thus, the beginning point is to understand something of God's desires and intentions, His divine design and purpose.

---

[9] George Barna, *The Power of Vision* (Ventura: Regal Books, 1992), 12.
[10] Ibid, 14.

CHAPTER 4

Authentic

That your faith … may be proved genuine.
—1 Peter 1:7

It is my understanding that bank tellers are taught to identify counterfeit currency by becoming familiar with authentic money. By knowing the feel, markings, and characteristics of real bills, they will know when a phony one is in their hands. It's a practice that can be applied to the church. There are so many different forms of heresies, false religions, alternative quests for God and pseudo forms of Christianity that to attempt to know all about them in order to avoid error would be overwhelming. Just as in detecting counterfeit money, the way to detect counterfeit religion is to become so familiar with the authentic version that counterfeit alternatives can be immediately identified.

How does one recognize the true church? What are the marks of authenticity that characterize a local church as genuine and not some kind of counterfeit version? As a pastor of a denominationally connected congregation, I am aware of the suspicions and questions many guests have when they first visit a new church. It is as if they have a checklist to evaluate whether or not it is really Christian. That approach is okay if the right questions are on the checklist. My suspicion is that many such litmus tests do not contain the most important questions. Perhaps that is because the general idea of "church" is often fuzzy, confused, and ill-defined in our culture. Images or models of the true church are as different as people's experiences or assumptions. A few of these images are worth mentioning here, primarily because they are common perceptions of the church, even though they fail to reflect the Messiah. Any version of the church that fails the Messiah test must be considered as counterfeit.

Perhaps the most common perception by people outside the church is that the church is, at root, mean-spirited. The evangelical version of the church is often portrayed by the popular media as being harsh, condemning, and hateful, which therefore produces guilt-ridden, emotionally damaged members. Unfortunately, some churches reinforce that perception by hateful and judgmental words and actions in the name of Christ. No doubt some of the antichurch sentiment reflects a perception scripted in their adolescent years. If, as a child, they were exposed to a legalistic, harsh, or mean experience in the church or its related institutions, their adult perception of the church can be negative and painful. Many have rejected the church in their adult years because they have experienced it as an organization devoid of grace and love. Sadly, that view of the church is shared by many people, whether Protestant, Catholic, or pagan, and is extremely difficult to overcome. Some congregations, in their desire to be biblical, risk falling into the pit of legalistic purity and, in so doing, reinforce the mean-spirited image of the church. It is a direct contradiction of what ought to be the vessel of grace and love that is presented in the scriptures.

Often for people active in the church, the power model is a common counterfeit version for congregational order. Patterned from the corporate pyramid system, the power-based church reflects the business approach to organizations in which a local congregation operates on some form of central authority and control. Power and control are especially dear to religious legalists. Those in positions of authority assume, and often claim, that they are operating according to the leading of the Spirit of God. The popularity of power religion is evidenced by the trend in many evangelical circles toward an elite, dominant group (often exclusively men) who control the life of a church through an exercise of centralized authority and power. This counterfeit model of the church has afflicted local congregations, denominations, and religious para-church organizations for centuries, resulting in numerous problems.

For one thing, it denies the Pentecostal experience. An authority/subject model abandons the concept of the church as a body in which every part is equal. Jesus's teaching and example was that the church, in method and message, is all about mutual surrender and servant love. It never should be based on any kind of mere human control and power. For an individual, or an elite few, to exercise any kind of power and control based on the assumption or claim that they have a special channel to God that sets them "above" or "over" others reveals an absence of trust in God and a refusal to surrender to the Holy Spirit. On the day of Pentecost all the people, including men and women, children and adults, Jews and gentiles, were anointed with power to serve. The nature of the church as inclusive instead of exclusive is illustrated by Paul's comparison of the church to the human body with an emphasis on the "less honorable parts" being given equal status with the more honorable parts (1 Corinthians 12).

Another counterfeit perception of the church that subtly infects many congregations is sometimes described as the "fortress mentality." As our postmodern world becomes more pluralistic and "gray," a blended paradigm replaces the definitive boundaries of traditional value norms (morals, lifestyle, family structure, etc.). The temptation to withdraw into religious cocoons in an attempt to feel safe and holy is very attractive. In the church it sometimes shows up in a return to doctrinal and theological statements of faith and membership requirements so that established boundaries will screen out of the church "corrupting sinners" (abortionists, homosexuals and feminists, etc.). While confessions of faith that identify the essential beliefs and distinctiveness of a congregation as well as some expectations of membership are valid and important, it is equally essential that such defining covenants reflect the authentic church as God's vessel of grace and not some form of pharisaical exclusivism. The danger is that congregational litmus tests can easily become a charter for a legalistic religion that builds "walls of hostility" (Ephesians 2:14) instead of a covenant of grace and love that builds bridges of redemption and healing. Thinking of the church as an exclusive enclave of holy people contradicts the divine image of Christ's open arms to those who are lost in the darkness with an invitation to enter into the light of God's love.

The fortress tendency continues to afflict some fellowships. While it is not limited to evangelical churches, it seems to be a particular temptation to them. The most common reaction is a defensive stance against those perceived as leftist theological liberal "marketplace" version churches. Fortress congregations see them as having a low view of scripture and high view of a melting-pot pluralism. Conversely, the reverse is also sometimes true. Liberal fortress-mentality churches view evangelicals as having a legalistic view of scripture and a low view of Christian love. The counterfeit church knows no theological, cultural, or philosophical boundaries as religious entities of all stripes can fall into the trap of false religion.

The "love-and-grace" standard for the church does not stand on the merits of exclusion or inclusion alone. The idea that to love is to accept and affirm everybody's lifestyle and beliefs as valid is not compatible with the biblical idea of love. Some behaviors are not appropriate, and some beliefs are not acceptable, primarily because they defame God and destroy people. The church's principal mode and message of love and grace are never understood or exercised apart from the person and message of Jesus Christ. To make love a standard for relationships without the grace of

Jesus Christ inevitably cheapens it into an approval of sin. Love is costly, holy and pure, as will be discussed later in this book. The exceptional nature of Christ-like love occurs when we love people without approving of their choices and beliefs. The purpose here is not to evaluate the error of either liberal or conservative churches but to expose the fallacy of any version of the church other than that which was preordained by God, founded on Christ, and empowered by the Holy Spirit. Any congregation that operates on an alternative vision, whether it be a fortress or marketplace view of the church will eventually experience disorder, conflict, and eventual division. Sometimes it comes as a violent shaking that divides the fellowship, although more often it is nothing more than an ignoring of the Spirit resulting in an absence of the Messiah awareness as people fade away and disappear into the secular world.

Today another paradigm of the church is emerging and impacting congregations of all descriptions: liberal, conservative, traditional, charismatic, denominational, and independent. It may best be described by the title of a popular secular magazine: *Self*. Reflecting the consumer mentality of our culture, the *Self* church's theology reflects the privatized, self-absorbed society in which we live, move, and have our beings. In this counterfeit version, the church is viewed as a place to "get a fix." The primary reason for its appeal is to have one's personal needs met in a way that leaves oneself in control while enhancing a good feeling. The unasked question is "what can I get?" instead of "how can I give?" People attend to be pampered. Consequently, the literature of the church is now created by specialists who produce slick marketing material that provide menus of services available. The first questions asked by church leaders is often "What do people want, and what are their felt needs?" not "What does God want?" The resulting impact on ministry design, facility construction, and worship form has been profound. The *Self* version of the church continues to radically impact the makeup of many congregations. Generational exclusive churches have effectively reached certain generations, but often do so at the expense of family unity. Families are often divided as the different generations attend different churches according to their "felt need." That generational exclusive nature of the self-focused church is not by accident but is the result of an agenda by some to reach those targeted generations. The question is, does it reflect the surrounding culture and its values, or does it reflect the value and agenda of Christ? Just because something is popular doesn't mean that it is in alignment with authentic spirituality.

When a church is founded on a false perception, there is lack of consistency. Many of the common perceptions of the church that were dominant a half century ago have faded as society has changed. The church as a hospital or as a social agency whose primary mission was to carry the torch for justice and social issues has faded. When was the last time a church established a medical facility? Those resources have been turned toward establishing Christian schools for the advantage of members' children. The decline of liberal theology and the rise of the political right, along with the impact of modern science that supports rather than contradicts biblical propositions,[11] continues to alter the landscape of religion in America.

The point of this discussion is not to give a detailed or exhaustive review of the many limited or distorted views that afflict the church, but to point out that we easily fall victim to

---

[11] Scientists, who have predominantly embraced evolutionary theory in the past, have been forced to embrace versions of origins of matter and life that agree with the theological propositions of Genesis: factual evidence for a sudden explosion of matter, called the Big Bang, involving at least ten dimensions (we live in a four-dimensional world); the indisputable evidence of a sudden appearance of species of life, rendering and the absence of any sustainable evidence of species transitioning; the unique DNA mathematical code of every living thing; etc. has caused many scientists to agree that there has to be a Designer. Some, who can't bring themselves to say "God," identify that agent as the "causer."

operating with a counterfeit understanding of what God intended. When we worship and serve with an inadequate understanding of the church, we inevitably develop a variety of dysfunctions that will, in time, result in conflict and division. Whenever that happens, the purpose and mission of the church is, at the very least, hindered and, at the worst, changed into a tool of destruction. The premise is twofold here. One is that the level of conflict and division in the church is evidence of a deep need for a renewed vision of what it means to be *the* church, the ekklesia.[12] The other is that errant versions of the church are perceived not by analyzing what is wrong with the church, but by holding up to the light the authentic vessel the Lord Jesus Christ called "my church." Such a new view begins with the purposes of God, purposes that were designed long before there was any heaven and earth.[13]

---

[12] The Greek word Jesus used that means "a called-out community."
[13] Ephesians 3:9–11.

CHAPTER 5

Design and Purpose

All the days ordained for me were written in your
book before one of them came to be.
—Psalm 139:16

When you travel down a road and see some stones stacked on top of a fence post, you know that it didn't happen by accident. First, the fence had to be built and placed there on purpose, and then someone had to place those stones there. What we may not know is why those rocks were balanced on that post. "Why?" is one of the most common questions asked by humans of God. Sometimes it is a cry of pain, as when disaster strikes or when we are the victim of an "accident." At other times we ask in a genuine search of the purposes of God. It should amaze us that God chooses to reveal himself to us at all, let alone give us insight into the mystery of his purposes. Yet he has chosen to do just that in a multitude of ways. The One who was "with God in the beginning" (John 1:2) promised, "Ask and it will be given to you; seek and you will find; knock and the door will be opened to you" (Matthew 7:7). Unfortunately, the problem is not in God's unwillingness to reveal the way, truth, and life to us.

The reason we often operate by counterfeit versions of meaning and purpose abides in our failure to ask, seek, or knock. Instead we pursue our personal agendas, somehow hoping that God will bless us so that in the end, His will aligns with our will. Unfortunately, we carry over into the church that same stumbling-in-the-dark mentality, bringing personal assumptions, expectations, and traditions to bear on the church. It creates a lose-lose situation, for when the church fails to fulfill our personal expectations, and it eventually will, then we feel wounded and often abandon her. This remains one of the primary causes of the disease that leads to conflict and decline in local congregations.

The divine process moves in a radically opposite flow. The a priori order for the revelation of God's will and purpose begins with the church. God's will for the individual is designed to be found in relationship to the community of believers, not vice versa. It is the church first, the individual second. Moreover it is in discovering the divine design and purpose for the church that one discovers personal meaning and fulfillment. It is a challenge in this individualistic me-first culture to lay aside personal agendas and to begin spiritual renewal through a focus on the church. Given the take-it-or-leave-it attitude that often seems to dominate people's stance toward a local church, it is radical in nature to suggest that personal renewal and healing begins with an understanding of the church Jesus intended. But that is how God ordained it. We are created to live in a community of faith. Even though we each have a personal relationship to Christ, it is nurtured, polished, and empowered in the context of a body of believers. Therefore, it seems that a crucial element in any renewal theology, whether it be for personal healing or congregational renewal, is to recapture a revelation of the *church*.

To understand the *church*, one must grasp the divine design and purpose that was ordained by God long before Jesus announced the ekklesia (the called-out people of God). Of the many characteristics of transcendent God, there are two that enable transient humans to know something of His divine nature. One is the discovery that God always operates by a design. The second is that He invades human history with a purpose. That

God acts by design and purpose is demonstrated in His works of creation and redemption, divine activities that provide fallen and redeemed humanity the opportunity to discover something of the mind and will of God. It is a revelation that can be experienced at all levels and stations in life, for it gives to us order, meaning, and hope for our personal lives, as well as for the church.

To believe that God is real is to accept the fact that He operates by design and purpose and that there is nothing in His realm that happens either accidentally or incidentally. Unlike His human creation, the Creator does not operate by chance. He does not fly by the seat of His divine pants, nor does He fail to see the end of all things, gambling on the outcome. Instead, His design and purpose are the constant forces in all facets of creation and life. This fact provides us with certain parameters that empower us to experience certain accomplishments. Whether sending astronauts into outer space or seeking the witness of his presence in the inner space of our mind, we are totally dependent upon the design and purpose that is constantly exercised by God.

The pioneers of modern-day science were able to develop usable theories of time and space because of their fundamental beliefs in God. The basic belief that there was an order to creation allowed pioneers of the scientific community to make essential discoveries about our universe. Confidence in the order of the universe gave definition to the laws and theorems of science in the form of boundaries and consistent results, which in turn provided the basis for the scientific and technological phenomena of our day. In studying the history of physical science, we find that people like Faraday, Newton, and Einstein, along with a multitude of other scientists past and present, were able to uncover the mysteries of natural law and order because they had confidence in the design and order of all things. It is that fundamental confidence that has allowed man to probe the wonders of both outer and inner space.

How ironic it is that contemporary science is often held hostage by a biological philosophy that is committed to the unsubstantiated principles of atheistic naturalism and accidental existence. Often more rooted in an agenda to eradicate belief in God than to uncover scientific fact, the empirical and unavoidable evidence of the Creator is rejected, compromising the historic basis of their "scientific" methodology. This manipulation by many of the intelligentsia of the world to conform the disciplines of science, law, and education to the tenets of random chance and natural selection exposes the critical importance of the church reflecting confidence in the God of design and purpose.[14] For if the church succumbs to the "reason" of antitheistic science, then there will be no revelation or answer to the "why" of life. If a holistic relationship to nature is rooted in the belief and experience that God created the universe with design and purpose, then it is both logical and reasonable to respond in the same manner to the other critical areas of our lives.

There are many issues of contemporary society today that reflect this basis of design and purpose, even in the absence of faith. Environmental causes that have become a global concern are promoted by an aggressive core of believers who perceive a necessary order in the natural cycles of species and nature. Whether it be the necessity of trees to sustain life on the planet or the cycle of salmon that return to a specific spawning bed on a certain river after thousands of miles of travel in the ocean, the environmentalist acts on the fundamental basis of design and order. The irony of our obsession with the environment is that those who are so motivated are usually motivated by a naturalistic principle while those who are theologically inspired are often not environmentally motivated. In view of the mandate to "fill the earth and subdue it ... rule over the fish of the sea and the birds of the air and over every living creature that moves on the ground" (Genesis 1:28), it seems that the Christian should be leading the

---

[14] Phillip E. Johnson, *Reason in the Balance* (Downers Grove; Inter Varsity Press, 1996) 193–204.

crusade for the care and maintenance of the planet and all that is contained therein. Instead, the church seems to be one of the last vestiges of society to deal with environmental concerns. That contradiction may be symptomatic of a problem existing in many churches, indicating a departure from the divine principle of design and purpose.

Human rights and the need for civil authority, justice, and order, which benefit both society and the individual, are also rooted in an understanding of the design and purpose of God, who has created us with "certain inalienable rights."[15] There are those who would interpret the "separation of church and state" as meaning that we must do away with anything that reflects or refers to the Judeo-Christian heritage of our laws and society. But history reveals that societies and governments that are based on premises other than the design and purpose of God inevitably result in chaos and anarchy. For that reason Paul's letter to the Romans makes submission to "every authority that exists"[16] an essential priority for all believers.

The preservation of the family and the institution of marriage are equally defined by God's design and purpose. The decline of the traditional home in American culture is marked by the increase of divorced parents and parallels the contemporary emphasis on the autonomous individual as the basis for defining society.[17] The divine design for the home and society is that of community where we are involved in both serving and receiving in order to be complete (Ephesians 5:21–28). When spouses discover the divine design of serving their mates, instead of expecting their mates to serve them, healing of the home begins to take place. It is

---

[15] United States Bill of Rights.

[16] Romans 13:1.

[17] Robert N. Bellah, *Habits of the Heart: Individualism and Commitment in American Life* (New York: Harper & Row, 1985). Bellah's work is an excellent review of the impact our obsession with individualism and autonomy is having on our culture, especially the home.

a biblical design that is revealed in the church and is to be applied to marriage, home, and society.

But the design and purpose of God is never more explicit and meaningful than in regard to the church. The church of Jesus Christ is both the object and the agent of God's design and purpose being fulfilled on earth. That is the impact of Paul's letters to the churches: "And God placed all things under his feet and appointed him to be head over everything for the church, which is his body, the fullness of him who fills everything in every way" (Eph. 1:22-23). It is impossible to understand Jesus Christ apart from His church, and conversely, one cannot conceive of the purpose and mission of the church apart from the person and work of Christ. While the church finds her source and purpose in Jesus Christ, His mission is completed through His church. Pentecost empowered the church to be the living presence (*His body*) of Christ on earth. Paul understood that the church is the final revelation of God and His agency for fulfilling His mission: "His intent was that now, **through the church**, the manifold wisdom of God should be made known to the rulers and authorities in the heavenly realms, according to his eternal purpose which he accomplished in Christ Jesus our Lord" (Ephesians 3:10–11). It is *through the church* that God's design and purpose is revealed and consummated.

The ultimate accomplishment of Christ is that through His work of redemption, He has destroyed the barriers that separate us from God and from one another, "the dividing wall of hostility" (Ephesians 2:14), bringing unity and peace—a reality God intended to be fulfilled in and through the church: "This mystery is that through the gospel the Gentiles are heirs together with Israel, members together of one body, and sharers together in the promise in Christ Jesus" (Ephesians 3:6). To understand the mission of Jesus Christ is to grasp the design and purpose of the church. To conceive of the significance of the church in God's purpose, it is necessary to understand the person and work of Christ. To experience a personal sense of mission so that the spending of personal resources of time, energy and finances begins with catching the divine vision and purpose for the church, the body of Christ.

CHAPTER 6

Predestined

Those God foreknew he also predestined to be
conformed to the likeness of his Son.
—Romans 8:29

Bob was a pilot in Vietnam forty years ago. Recently he was part
of a group who visited Asia on a cruise ship. Included in the ship's
itinerary was a stop in Da Nang, where he had been based during
the war. There he had worked closely with a Vietnamese officer,
who had become his best friend. Often Bob had been invited into
this man's home, where he had been accepted as one of the family.
After the collapse of Saigon and the war's end, he'd never heard
from his friend. Sailing into the harbor brought mixed emotions of
pleasant memories and an overwhelming sense of pain and grief.
He told the rest of his party that he would stay on board while they
went ashore to see the city.

But at the last minute, he left the ship, only instead of boarding
the tour bus, he hailed a cab. Bob decided he wanted to go to the
home of his friend to see if it was still there or if any of his friend's
family were still alive. He got into the cab and stared at the cab
driver with stunned unbelief. The cab driver was his long lost
friend. After the war he had been sent to a communist reeducation
camp for four years. Now, even though he was a college-educated
man, because he was "the enemy" during the war, he will never be

allowed to do anything more than drive a cab. Bob's friend drove to the old family home, where he had a grand reunion with other members of the family.

The odds against these two men meeting like that after thirty years are so great one wonders if it wasn't predestined by God. Out of the many taxi drivers at the dock that day, that Bob would enter the one driven by his longtime friend is truly phenomenal. Suddenly, the punishment of being only a cab driver became a blessing.

Whether it was coincidence or divine intervention that those two men met that day, I do not know. Some people see God's hand in every incident of their personal lives, while others wait for a "sign" from God to validate their faiths. There are many unexplained coincidences in life, and there are many instances that can only be explained by divine intervention. Certainly, to understand something of the sovereignty of God demands that He is able and often willing to enter into human history in order to fulfill His purpose. It not only stands to reason, but also it is theologically sound to believe that behind some of life's mysteries and surprises are God's intervention and care.

For example, I believe that it is no accident that the church is still alive after two thousand years. Given the mistakes, corruption, and persecution throughout the centuries, it would be understandable if the church had gone the way of many ancient and powerful empires over the same stretch of time. Yet in spite of the opposition and her failures, the church not only still stands, but also it continues to be the singular God-ordained agency for proclamation of the gospel of grace to the world. That is as God planned. This divine plan for the church is couched in the scriptural language of predestination and election: "For those God foreknew he also predestined to be conformed to the likeness of his Son, that he might be the firstborn among many brothers. And those he predestined, he also called; those he called, he also justified; those he justified, he also glorified" (Romans 8:29–30).

"Firstborn" refers to the unique new creation that is brought about by the resurrection of Christ, which resulted in the new "people of God." Ancient Israel, the original "people of God," was a religious/political/social entity that was limited to one basic ethnic group (Jews) who occupied one geographical area (Palestine) and who were held together by a common tradition (Egypt and Sinai). They understood *firstborn* as a symbolic word for their deliverance from slavery by a blood sacrifice, referring to the final plague in Egypt that resulted in their escaping bondage. In time they came to understand that it was part of God's plan promised to Abraham centuries earlier. It appears that they came to think of "predestined to be God's chosen people" to mean that they were invincible, no matter what. What they failed to comprehend was that the predetermined plan of God for *Israel* transcended their land, nation, and law. It was merely a precursor of the "people of God" who were to come. The "new Israel" would be a people in which "there is neither Jew nor Greek, slave nor free, male nor female" (Galatians 3:28). Paul further defines the people "born from among the dead" as the church, which, like ancient Israel, is delivered by the "firstborn," a reference to Christ: "And he is the head of the body, the church; he is the beginning and the firstborn from among the dead, so that in everything he might have the supremacy" (Colossians 1:18).

While the scriptures do not use the title "new Israel" for the church, there are many passages that refer to the church as "the people of God." Paul goes to great length in Romans to help Jewish Christians understand the expanded meaning of "the people of God." He defines them as one, Jew and Gentile, who embrace Christ by faith. Abraham, the father of faith, was credited by God as righteous because of his faith a half millennium before the law was given at Sinai. A similar message is found in the letter to the church at Galatia. "Understand, then, that those who believe are children of Abraham" (Galatians

3:7). Peter uses the essential characteristics of ancient Israel to describe the persecuted and scattered church made up of both Jew and Gentile: "But you are a chosen people, a royal priesthood, a holy nation, a people belonging to God, that you may declare the praises of him who called you out of darkness into his wonderful light. Once you were not a people, but now you are the people of God; once you had not received mercy, but now you have received mercy" (1 Peter 2:9–10). Titus refers to the church as "a people that are his very own" (Titus 2:14), and in Ephesians we read, "You are no longer foreigners and aliens, but fellow citizens with God's people and members of God's household" (Ephesians 2:19).

God's predestined purpose in choosing Israel to be his people has profoundly impacted the Jewish people throughout history and continues to do so today. Our American diplomatic process is influenced by that "predestined" understanding of modern Israel. In the church, most end-time Armageddon scenarios revolve around God's predestined purpose for Israel. Whether these prophecies are literal or spiritual, symbolic or historic, is open for much debate. What is not open for debate is the fact that God's eternal purposes and salvation history are wholly vested in the church. It could be that Israel might be defined in modern times as a player in apocalyptic events of the future, but it surely will not be so at the demise of the church. It is the church that is identified as the "bride of Christ." It is the church that is raptured to eternal status. It is the church that is the object of God's predestined plan. Grasp something of the divine purpose for the church, and it will radically impact how one worships, serves, and relates to the world .

Unfortunately, church history is to some degree defined by conflict and division over what is meant by predestination and election. It is interesting that the word *predestined* occurs only four times in the Bible, twice each in Romans and Ephesians, but those references have been a theological monolith since early on in the church.[18] Of the various differences that characterize the theological watershed that divide the major groups of Protestantism, none is more defining than the positions taken over the meaning of predestination. The word *elect* appears eleven times, all in the New Testament, with all usages but one a synonym for "the church." The word *preordained* does not appear in the Bible, while *ordained* is used thirteen times in the Old Testament and only once in the New Testament, when Jesus quotes Psalm 8:2.[19] The idea of predestination has often been understood in terms of "who is elected and who is not" according to what God has foreordained. Making "who" the focus of election and predestination is man-centered, not Christ-centered, and can result in the practice of exclusivity, separatism, prejudice, and even atrocities against those deemed "nonelect."[20] It remains one of the characteristics of fallen people, that the gospel of grace, which was ordained of God to bring unity and peace, becomes the tool for division and acrimony. When that happens it is blasphemy to call that gathering a "church," for it has nothing to do with the divine purpose and has, in fact, become the enemy of the body of Christ.

One of the essential precreation plans by God involves the church. Paul's letter to the Ephesians reveals that the Creator preordained that he would reveal his person and purpose to the nations of the world through the church. Paul understood that the same grace God extended to him, resulting in his being

---

[18] J. D. Douglas, "Augustine of Hippo," in *The New International Dictionary of the Christian Church*, (1978; Grand Rapids: Zondervan). Augustine's views on election and predestination were fermented in the midst of controversy and have remained the primary reference point in contemporary circles of theological debate today.

[19] Matthew 21:16.

[20] The establishment of Massachusetts Bay Colony on the basis of religious freedom was a sham as it soon became evident that those who differed from the official form and doctrine were not accepted as elect and were punished, expelled, or put to death. Modern forms of such thinking are behind some of the atrocities in places like South Africa and Ireland.

forgiven and then called to be an apostle, is the mystery that God preordained for the church to reveal to the nations. "Although I am less than the least of all God's people, this grace was given me: to preach to the Gentiles the unsearchable riches of Christ, and to make plain to everyone the administration of this mystery, which for ages past was kept hidden in God, who created all things. His intent was that now, through the church, the manifold wisdom of God should be made known to the rulers and authorities in the heavenly realms, according to his eternal purpose which he accomplished in Christ Jesus our Lord" (Ephesians 3:8–11). The church is God's unique, ordained vessel of grace to the world. It was designed and established in the mind of the Creator before he ever said, "Let there be." In simple language, the Creator's precreation plan included the church as the ultimate expression of His self-revelation and redemption program.

How God would make final His redemptive plan remained a mystery in prechurch history. Israel, as the people of God with their law, temple, and promised land, was the first visible revelation of God outside of that which is evidenced in the wonders of nature. But Israel, as a nation-state-people of God, was not the final revelation of the people of God. Although a magnificent and strategic part of God's salvation history for the world, she was not ordained or designed to be the ultimate identification of his being. Her purpose was to provide the setting for the Messiah, Jesus Christ, who would bring into existence the ultimate revelation of God, which is His church. "His intent was that now, through the church, the manifold wisdom of God should be made known" (Ephesians 3:10). Everything that Israel was as God's vessel was poured into the new covenant and expanded through Christ and His church. God is exposed for who and what He is through grace, not the law.

Amazing as it may seem, especially given the failures, corruption, conflict, and shallow political alliances of the church through her history, God chose to put all His eggs in that one basket. There is nothing in scripture indicating that God had a plan B in case the church would not work out. It is through the *church* universal, made up of Jews and Gentiles (all kinds and nations of people) who have surrendered to Christ Jesus as Redeemer and Lord. It is through the *church*, universal and local, expressed in the evangelizing, nurturing, healing, sending activities that God is fulfilling His salvation plan for the world. Perhaps few, if any, congregations realize the pre-eternal, unique, and mysterious purposes of God being poured into their gatherings.

When we set aside preconceived notions and theological scripts that were written to indoctrinate, and sort through all the biblical texts and other contexts regarding election and predestination, we should come to the realization that those theologically charged words really are about God's design and purpose for the church. Theological issues and interpretations of predestination and election in regard to the individual are secondary. The application for the believer in the church is to understand God's purpose and design for the church and then find a place to serve. The contemporary spiritual trend of privatizing everything so that it is about "me," including even God's preordained purpose, is an abuse of scripture and another example of our egocentric theology.

Paul indicated that personal predestination is about becoming more like Christ so that together we can be effective participants in His church: "For those God foreknew he also predestined to be conformed to the likeness of his Son" (Romans 8:29). Biblically healthy and spiritually whole congregations come to understand that our personal divine purpose emerges to the degree that we become part of the body of Christ. The foreknowledge of God remains unknown except to the extent that the "elect" become conformed to the image of Jesus Christ. In that light it can be reasonably argued that only through the process of being the church do we discover and fulfill the design and purposes of God. The ability to know God's precreation mind transcends humanity's capability: "Who has known the mind of the Lord?

Or who has been his counselor?" (Romans 11:34). Our knowledge of the mind of the Lord is limited to what God has chosen to reveal to us through His Son, our Savior, Jesus Christ. Predestination, and all that it implies, is then moved from the tenets of doctrinal definition into the arena of practical ecclesiology. The church is subsequently identified not by her ability to know and understand the precreation mind of God but by the exercising God's spiritual gifts so that, together, her people become the fulfillment of God's design and purpose to bring healing to the world.

CHAPTER 7

Sin and Division

The wages of sin is death.
—Romans 6:23

W hen theology and doctrine create division rather than unity in the church, the precise opposite of the design and purpose of God is being implemented, resulting in a distortion of the image of Christ. The identification of the elect is revealed in how they reflect the truth of Christ by conforming to His image, being driven by the same motivation that propelled Him to fulfill His mission.[21] Being aware that God operates with design and purpose provides us with a solid foundation for a multitude of endeavors, a reason for hope, and a mandate for how we function as His people. That mandate is summed up in the phrase "to know and to do the will of God." As Ray Anderson states, "knowing" has to do with *orthodoxy* (right knowledge) and "doing" has to do with *orthopraxy* (right practice).[22]

There seem to be two common failures in this regard. One is to focus so much on "knowing" that there develops an *orthodoxy*

---

[21] Philippians 2:6–11 is a New Testament hymn parallel to the Suffering Servant in Isaiah 53. The preface verses of 1–5 are the point of the hymn— that the believers are to be driven by the same purpose.

[22] Ray S. Anderson, *Ministry on the Fireline*, (Pasadena: Fuller Seminary, 1995), 168.

without any *orthopraxy*. It was one of the many problems posed by the intrusion of gnosticism in the early church. To the Gnostics, knowledge was all that mattered, rendering motive and behavior as of no concern. Such a belief system not only leads to moral corruption and social abuses but also deletes the need for grace. Knowledge of what is right that does not lead to doing the right thing is not only wasted information but also is a form of rejecting God. It threatened the viability of the early church, prompting James to write, "Anyone, then, who knows the good he ought to do and doesn't do it, sins (hamartia) " (James 4:17). To understand the design and purpose of God and fail to act upon it is to choose a different god, which is to fall into the sin of idolatry.

An essential purpose for the body of Christ has to do with understanding the deeper nature of sin, especially in light of grace. It is one thing to understand sin in relationship to the law of Moses, a judicial paradigm in which the slightest violation of the rule constitutes sin. It is another thing to understand sin in light of the grace of Jesus Christ. Both have moral implications and, therefore, impact one's relationship with God and with others. Both reveal the unworthiness of fallen humans exposed by the holiness of God. Both depend upon atonement and redemption by a power apart from one's own ability and might. But there is a significant difference between the two realms of law and grace. If establishing a law with a set of rules while exercising a judicial system of justice on those who are guilty of sin would solve the problem, then Jesus did not have to come, suffer, and die as the atonement for sin. Essential to understanding the church as God's ordained vessel of grace is to grasp the root nature of sin, why it is condemned, and how it plays out in our attitude toward God. Failure to understand sin results in failure to experience grace.

While there are many nuances to the usage and meaning of "sin" in the Bible, its most basic is that of hamartia, usually interpreted as "missing the mark."[23] To sin (hamartia) is to live with the wrong focus. To put one's sights on any target other than the person and purpose of God is to commit hamartia. It takes on many forms in our private spiritual journey as well as in our church fellowship. The congregation that splits over which kind of music to sing is guilty of hamartia, for they have taken their focus off of God and his will and have moved style of music into the center. The same is true of any issue that becomes more important than the unity of the fellowship, leading to division. Such an issue, righteous or unrighteous as it may be, has become more important than the fulfillment of God's design and order and has been made to stand above Christ's plea for unity, which results in the exercise of grace. When God is denied His rightful place as both our source and object, and life is pursued by criteria other than that of fulfilling God's purpose, we are guilty of hamartia—we have missed the mark. However it is expressed, in desire or deed, belief or behavior, hamartia is refusing to recognize the status, character, and claims of God and, as such, is a denial and rejection of Him, usually in favor of oneself.

For Paul, the "self assertion against the claim of God"[24] is nothing less than the continuation of original sin. The failure to submit to God, which is the nerve center of every individual sin, always results in separation, the ultimate expression of which is death.[25] The purpose of revelation is to give us knowledge about the design and purpose of God so that we can "do" his will and avoid falling into hamartia. Jesus Christ, "the image of the invisible God," (Colossians 1:15) is the ultimate revelation of that divine design and purpose. Knowledge of God's will is therefore more than information; it involves a lifestyle that is deliberately lived by focusing on the design and purpose of God. When believers are

---

[23] Gerhard Kittel, *Theological Dictionary of the New Testament*, Volume 1, (Grand Rapids: Eerdmans, 1987), 267–316.

[24] Romans 7:14–25.

[25] Kittel, 310.

motivated accordingly, then they *are* the elect, and they focus on conforming to the image of Christ.

Another common errant focus is to misinterpret the design and purpose of God so that we opt for a lesser mission, or one that is an aberration of the real mission, causing the individual, or the church, to miss the mark (hamartia). A classic example is the focus in many evangelical circles on accumulation of knowledge of the "inerrant" scriptures, while failing to make the truth of the scriptures infallible. Inerrancy is concerned with the technical validation of the original writings, while infallibility has to do with the eternal meaning and impact of the truth. While arguing about inerrancy, some people become exclusive, judgmental, and divisive in the church—a contradiction of the healing intent of the work of grace in Christ and the purpose of the church. To change the text of the gospel of reconciliation into a tool that destroys and divides the fellowship is unthinkable. Such hamartia falls into the kind of sin strongly denounced by Jude.[26] That is because the mission of Christ and the mandate to the church is not about judgment and exclusion, but about redemption effected through the processes of repentance, renewal, and restoration. The purpose of the Great Command (Mark 12:29–31) and the Great Commission (Matthew 28:18–20) is that the church will continue Christ's mission of healing and liberation.

Perhaps a reason for the frequent loss of vision in the church and a consequent failure to understand and fulfill God's design and purpose is directly related to a decline in Christian literacy.

---

[26] Jude 4–19 is one of the most scathing descriptions of those who deny Christ and in so doing lead the believer away from God. The final observation is that there are those who "divide you, who follow mere natural instincts and do not have the Spirit." His descriptions of them are some of the most dramatic in scripture: they are "blemishes at your love feasts, shepherds who feed only themselves ... clouds without rain, blown along by the wind; autumn trees, without fruit and uprooted, twice dead ... wild waves of the sea, foaming up their shame; wandering stars, for whom blackest darkness has been reserved forever."

While there is limited supportive data, it seems that the average person sitting in the pew is without the historical-biblical context of earlier generations. It is not difficult to understand how media sound bites has impacted the church.[27] Some elements of the church-growth movement are designed to facilitate a similar mode in worship. Richard John Neuhaus calls it a shameless promotion of "turning worship into entertainment and the congregation into an audience."[28] Perhaps such dramatization of worship can be defended on the basis of the literacy level of some of the generations returning to the church. The irony is that declining Christian literacy comes at the very point in history when the dissemination of both the Word of God and books on spirituality are unparalleled. With the proliferation of books, the availability of video and movie versions of Bible stories, audio cassettes, and now the presence of computer applications, never has there been so much exposure available to the average church member. Most homes have at least a family Bible, and most believers have several different versions of the Bible, including new, contemporary paraphrased editions. Study Bibles proliferate, and the church-growth movement has spawned small-group studies in homes. Yet there appears to be a declining knowledge of the fundamental truth of the Word of God, or in many cases, an alternative "knowledge" that for some has replaced the more fundamental truth of God's self-revelation.

Hamartia also often plagues the church with a view that the message of Christ is designed to appeal to and appease individuals rather than to present them with an opportunity to understand the design and purpose of God so that there is transformation into the image of Christ. The inspired affirmation of God's purpose in Christ, that we might "be conformed to the likeness of his Son"

---

[27] Neil Postman, *Amusing Ourselves to Death* (New York: Penguin, 1985), 114–124.

[28] Richard John Neuhaus, *Freedom for Ministry* (Grand Rapids: Eerdmans, 1992), 137.

(Romans 8:29), is often reversed, so that we begin to expect Him to conform to our wants. Some people abandon the church and reject God because they did not get what they wanted or did not feel like they deserved a disaster that struck. It is a major form of hamartia in that the call to become a unique people of God is aborted in favor of a religion of the self. There is nothing unique about people who accept or reject God based on personal desires. The result is confusion, contradiction, and, too often, conflict within the fellowship of believers. The ekklesia can survive only by a focus on the will of God. Any other driving force, goal, objective, motivation, or agenda is hamartia and will ultimately bring chaos, confusion, conflict, division, and damage to people desperate for the healing touch of Christ. Healing is what it is all about: "The wages of sin is death, but the gift of God is eternal life in Christ Jesus our Lord" (Romans 6:23).

CHAPTER 8

Ekklesia

I will build my church.
—Matthew 16:18

What makes a church a *church*? Just because a group of people legally charter a nonprofit religious corporation, hang out a sign, and hold worship services does not mean that it is a *church* in the eyes of God. Just because a church is aligned with a parent denomination, or for some is *not* so aligned, does not mean it is a *church*. Just because a building is called a church and people do religious activities in it does not mean it is a *church*. Just because a congregation grows in numbers and has the best production in town, does not mean it is a *church*. Just because a congregation has only "sanctified" or "holy" or "good" people in it (suggesting that they have successfully weeded out the undesirables) does not mean it is a *church*. And just because a congregation maintains an absence of conflict does not mean that it is a *church*.

Conversely, just because it experiences conflict and division does not mean it no longer is a *church*. The difference between church and *church* is significant. By church I mean a religious institution that has *a form of godliness* but is not necessarily operating according to the *power of His Spirit* (2 Tim. 3:5). Churches may have buildings, bylaws and organizational structures, hold worship services, conduct fellowship activities, and carry out religious functions. But having and doing all those things does not mean that it is a *church*.

By *church*, I am referring to a gathering of people whose primary purpose is to know and do God's will. It is an assembly of people not only grounded in the Word of God but also living by the power of the Holy Spirit, a congregation of redeemed sinners who are keenly aware that they are both objects and vessels of God's grace, a body of servants who submit to one another because they have surrendered their hearts to God. It is a fellowship whose power to change lives is love and submission, not the power of authority and control commonly exercised in the world. It is a place where the primary issue is to celebrate Jesus Christ as Savior and Lord, a covenant of believers who are transformed into a vessel of grace where lost and wounded people experience the living presence of the resurrected Messiah.

A scan of today's religious landscape reveals that there are many definitions, as well as unsubstantiated assumptions, as to what constitutes a *church*. Many are derivatives or substitutes, but not biblical identities, of the *church*. Likewise, the evidence indicates that confusion over identity is one of the issues that leads to conflict, decline, and division of congregations. The result is spiritual wounding of believers. Therefore, any theology for the healing of wounded congregations must include a clear understanding of the authentic *church*.

The first order is to grasp what God predestined and designed that His Son, Jesus Christ, established. When Peter confessed that Jesus was the Anointed Christ, the Son of God, the maker and master of everything, Jesus responded, "I will build my *church* and the gates of Hades will not overcome it" (Matt. 16:18). Because of the history of the church, the play on the Greek word *petra* (rock) has been the focus of most exegesis of this passage. If it is concluded that the point of His comment was Peter, then a system of human authority and power will serve as the basis of the church. However, if Jesus was announcing the "church" based on

Peter's confession as understanding the new "people of God," then what follows is based not on human authority, but on the power of confession and trust in Jesus. The answer is found in the rest of the story, as scripture becomes its own interpreter. The events and inspired teaching that follow in the gospels and the letters give definition and direction for the *church*, not Peter.

The important significance of that conversation between the disciples and Jesus, as they watched the idolatrous worship taking place where the springs emerged out of the mountain to begin the Jordan River, was his announcement of the *church*. The word he used for *church* was not unfamiliar to the disciples. *Ekklesia* was a common Greek word used to describe a public gathering. It had not previously been used to denote the people of God who gathered for worship. It was a revelation. Traditionally, the gathering of people in the synagogue was exclusive not public. Only Jews were allowed into the temple, whereas ekklesia was public and included all kinds of people. It was an indication of the radical inclusion and diversity that would mark the *church*. God takes that which is common—people of all kinds who are common sinners—and by His grace and power transforms them into His great and ultimate vessel of grace and healing (i.e., the *church*). To use the word ekklesia was to identify a radical new wineskin as the vessel for the new wine (Luke 5:38).

The unusual and yet common word not only spoke to the makeup of the church but also indicated the function of the people. Ekklesia is a compound word made up from *ek* meaning "out," and *klesis* "to call." Throughout church history, ekklesia has been understood to refer to those who are called out by God. Unfortunately, some churches and religious sects have understood that to mean that to be a Christian requires separation from the world in a way in which they no longer are involved in the normal affairs of life. After all, so the reasoning goes, Paul admonished the church at Corinth to not be "yoked together with unbelievers," to "come out from among them and be separate," and to "touch no unclean thing" (2 Cor. 6:14–18). And Jesus in his parable of the sheep and goats in Matthew 25:31–46 refers to God separating people "from one another as a shepherd separates the sheep from the goats."

Such an understanding of the nature of the church is the result of misunderstanding both the scripture and the intent of Jesus, who, instead of separating his disciples from the world, sent them into the world. A more careful analysis of both references commonly used to define the church as a people separated from society is necessary. The parable by Jesus mentioned above is about postchurch events, looking forward to the moment when all humanity will stand before the judgment throne. It is at the point, after his return and the ekklesia is removed from the world, that a separatism will be put into effect. In fact, a more careful look at the parable reveals it is not about believers being called apart from the world but about the necessity of our being involved in the world. The reason for the divine judgment of separating sheep from goats is determined by whether or not there was involvement as the ekklesia in the lives of people. After all, are not the primary driving issues of life among the nations, the marketplace, the defense programs, and the politics of communities, ultimately about food, shelter, and clothing? Instead of this being a text to support the ekklesia as a people "called apart from the world," it is a convicting parable of Jesus calling his *church* to become more involved in the world around them.

Likewise, it is important to understand the cultural setting of Paul's admonition to the Corinthians to practice separatism. The issue was their tendency to combine Christian faith and practice with pagan belief and idolatry. Like lighting a match to check the contents of a gasoline tank, blending faith in God and worship of false gods can only result in disaster. The unclean thing they must not touch is the belief that any object, teaching, religious order, or activity, other than the grace of God, can make them holy or provide for their needs. Trusting in God's grace, depending on salvation through Christ alone, and obeying the leading of the Holy Spirit are the only means of salvation and security. It, therefore, must remain the basis for individual and corporate priorities and values. To mix into Christian faith any of the world's value system is deadly and is ultimately a denial of the redemption of Christ and the sovereignty of God.

It has always been a temptation for believers to try to blend worldly priorities with Christian commitment. Nothing has changed for the contemporary church. We easily fall into the mental fog of wanting God's blessing apart from total surrender to Him. So we call on Him but then seek to secure our lives by the means of the world. People today who consider themselves good Christians but who live by a value system rooted more in Hollywood than in the Holy Bible are modern versions of the Corinthian malaise. Likewise, the number of pew sitters who believe in naturalism (belief that everything comes from the biological, geophysical, and chemical activity of nature—as in Darwin's evolutionary theory) instead of faith in theism (the belief that everything comes from God) are called on to decide in whom or what they believe. The separation called for in Corinth is a pulling out not from normal living interaction in the world but from the pattern of the world in terms of *why* and *how* one interacts with society. It's a separating of the soul and mind and heart from the influences of a carnal agenda so that confidence, trust, and hope are in God alone.

That, then, becomes the basis for a more effective and meaningful involvement by the church in the surrounding culture. Someone has compared the church to a ship that belongs in the sea. Problems arise when the sea enters into the ship. The call then, to be separate, is an issue of identity for the purpose of bringing the community of believers into relationship with God so that they are effective agents of grace in the world.

That brings us back to consideration of the ekklesia. There is an alternative interpretation that begs our attention. Instead of limiting our understanding of ekklesia to "being *called out* of the world," it can be accurately translated to mean to *call out* to the world." God's people are those who call out to the world the good news of Jesus Christ. That fits with the whole of scripture, beginning with the incarnation of Christ. In John 17:18 Jesus prays, "As you sent me into the world, I have sent them into the world." If He was promoting the idea that his people would be *called out* from the world, He never would have come as a man. Philippians 2:6–8 would never be written: "Who (Jesus), being in very nature God, did not consider equality with God something to be grasped, but made himself nothing, taking the very nature of a servant, being made in human likeness. And being found in appearance as a man, he humbled himself and became obedient to death—even death on a cross!" (Philippians 2:6–8)

To be the ekklesia is Jesus's mandate to his followers to continue being the living presence of God incarnate in the world. Luke records the Lord's final words to his disciples that "repentance and forgiveness of sins will be preached in his name to all nations" (Luke 24:47). That is a *proclamation* mandate, not a *privatized* separatist activity. The Great Commission in Acts 1:8 commissions us to be his "witnesses in Jerusalem, and in all Judea and Samaria, and to the ends of the earth." Again, that requires our being involved in the world in order to *call out* the good news. Mark 16:15 gives Jesus's postresurrection directive to his followers: "He said to them, 'Go into all the world and preach the good news to all creation" *(Mark 16:15)*. That hardly sounds like a separated-from-the-world kind of commission. Instead it is the mandate to proclaim, to *call out*, to the world the riches of God's grace and love.

Ekklesia—the *church*—is God's preordained vessel of grace, the living body of Christ, who continues his work of bringing light into darkness. Ekklesia means to be out among the broken, wounded dying people of the world, extending to all the healing power of Christ for redemption, restoration, and renewal. Ekklesia is the living Word that calls out to a frightened, terrorized people in darkness the message of hope and peace. The ekklesia is God's unique, preordained vessel of grace anointed by the Holy Spirit to announce, administer and activate the good news of the forgiveness of sins by the blood of Jesus.

Part II

The Healing Process

Chapter 9

The Healing Mission

I have come that they may have life, and have it to the full.
—John 10:10

It was a golden fall day. Cliff, my brother-in-law, was driving his pickup truck as we moseyed down a country road through wheat stubble fields in eastern Oregon. Our destination was a certain field in which to hunt ring-neck pheasants. The journey through the fields was a hunt in itself, as at any time the elusive bird might be spotted. Some movement in a field caught my eye, and I asked him to stop. I stepped over the barbed wire fence and walked out into the field, coming upon a most unusual sight. A large owl and a gopher were locked in a deadly circle. The owl had obviously swooped down and grabbed the gopher with its large, powerful talons. But the gopher, in a panic reaction, had turned and bitten the owl. Its sharp, curved front teeth had penetrated through and locked on the upper beak of the owl. The gopher was dead—rigor mortis had set in. But because the owl had a death grip on the body of the dead gopher, and the gopher had a death grip on its upper beak, the owl's head was pulled down so that it could not fly. The motion I had spotted was the owl attempting to fly.

Because of the large wingspan, and memories of being flogged by a large wild goose as a young boy, I carefully picked up the unusual pair locked in a circle of death and carried them over to the pickup. To my surprise, the owl never struggled or offered any resistance. While I sat on the tailgate holding the owl, Cliff gently but firmly pulled the owls talons free from the body of the dead gopher. Then, using his pocket knife, he pried open the gopher's mouth until the beak of the owl was released, and the dead gopher carcass dropped to the ground.

The owl was free but made no effort to fly. As I sat and held that beautiful bird, it just looked at me with those round, brown eyes, never once struggling to be free. We discussed whether or not it would be able to fly or if we would have to take it to someone who could nurture it back to health. Finally, I carried it some distance and set it down on the ground beside the road. We sat on the tailgate watching our liberated bird, waiting for it to fly away. It didn't move, and after considerable time, we concluded that it was too weak to do so and that we would have to take it to someone who could care for it. I started to walk toward it when it suddenly spread its wings and lifted off the ground. It flew low over the field below us, circling and gaining altitude, and then soared right over the top of us, disappearing over a low ridge. I expected it to dip its wings. We both stood in stunned silence for some time. My mind was immediately filled with the cry of Paul in Romans 7:24: "Who will rescue me from this body of death?"

To answer the critical question, "What is God's design and purpose for the church?" we turn to the Master, for His life is a model, His teaching is a mandate, and His atonement is the medium of His design and purpose for the church. When Jesus began His public ministry, He announced his mission. Luke recorded that He went to the Synagogue, where He was handed the scroll to read. He read from the prophet Isaiah: "The Spirit of the Lord is on me, because he has anointed me to preach good news to the poor. He has sent me to proclaim freedom for the prisoners and recovery of sight for the blind, to release the oppressed, to proclaim the year of the Lord's favor" (Luke 4:18–19).

What Jesus meant by *freedom, recovery,* and *release* is open for interpretation, as well as who is meant by the *poor*, the *prisoners*, the *blind*, and the *oppressed*. No doubt He had a greater vision than Isaiah had when penning those words under the Spirit's influence. While Isaiah's context and meaning is significant, it is more important to understand what Jesus meant, for how that pronouncement is deciphered becomes a critical issue for the church. While Isaiah was envisioning the healing of the nation of Israel, Jesus was aware of the grasp sin and death has on all humanity and how in our blindness we clutch tightly to that which is destroying us. His interpretation of Isaiah's words is demonstrated in a brief but profound ministry of healing and liberation. Healing is the dominant focus of His ministry. It was prophesied by the Psalmist: He "forgives all your sins and heals all your diseases" (Psalm103:3). Whether it was physical, spiritual, relational, or social bondage, His acts and words were a prying loose from the individual the grip of sin and death, setting free the individual so that he or she could "soar on wings like eagles" (Isaiah 40:31).

The significance of His announcement of a ministry of healing and liberating must not be casually dismissed. Too often in church history, it has been set aside in favor of moralistic (legalistic), systematic (theological), and didactic (doctrinal) reductions. While everything Jesus did and said has implications for those important facets of the faith, His mission is to bring healing to men and women who are created in the image of God but who are trapped in a circle of sin and death.

The healing theme of Jesus's ministry provides the essential focus for the church. It is a critical issue, for whatever is the focal point of a congregation will drive the ministry forms for that community of believers. If it is an alternative focus other than what Jesus had for ministry, then the result will be different from one of healing and liberation. Jesus defines the primary ministry of the church as one of healing, of setting free those who are trapped in the various forms of bondage to sin and death. When the body of believers exercises the same kind of love exhibited by the life and death of Christ, they not only experience personal fulfillment and a sense of righteousness, but also they become God's ordained agents of healing. Conversely, when the ministry of the church is centered on something other than healing and liberation, then not only will wounded people be neglected, but also congregations will fall prey to alternative agendas, often becoming battlefields, a condition which seems to be at epidemic proportions today.

Some of the common issues that have historically dominated the focus of the church and that are at the center of much of contemporary evangelicalism that seriously threaten the viability and mission of the church are *doctrinal nationalism, political evangelism,* and *spiritual uniformity.* They become a circle of death, trapping the fellowship with worldly talons as dedicated people hang on for dear life to causes and issues, thinking that they will experience deliverance from death. They are worldly and deadly because they revolve around exercising power and control, not submission and serving, a contradiction to any reasonable interpretation of Jesus's mission. As Darrell Guder points out in discussing the problem of reductionism, we attempt "to reduce the gospel, to bring it under control, to render it intellectually respectable, or to make it serve another agenda than God's purposes."[29]

Doctrinal nationalism is the hamartia (sin) of identifying the kingdom of God with a national entity, transposing the favored status of Israel under the old covenant onto a particular nation under the new covenant. More than one Western national entity has assumed an image of divine favor of this nature. To do so, doctrine and prophecy is interpreted through a nation-centric rather than a Christ-centric perspective.[30] It seems that one of the inevitable results of doctrinal nationalism is that religious

---

[29] Darrell L. Guder, *The Continuing Conversion of the Church,* Eerdmans, p. 102.
[30] House and Ice, pp. 30–31

righteousness is merged with political power. A major paradigm of the Messiah carried by most Israelites was that when He would appear He would overthrow the Roman oppressors and return the nation Israel to dominant political power. Today's movement by evangelicals into the political stream of America carries the grave danger of making the same mistake. But power politics was never even close to the ways and means of Jesus. While followers of Christ are called to be model citizens, rendering to Caesar what is Caesar's, including serving the community through political office and being involved in the civil order, it is critical that the church is never identified with any political party or agenda and that the mission of the church not be reduced to social or political issues. Confusing patriotism with religion has repeatedly corrupted and conflicted the church through her two-thousand-plus years of history.

Whenever church and state (or church and anti-state) are synonymous, the healing ability of the church is not only diminished, if not lost, but also becomes an agent of wounding citizens. The agenda for the church must never be set by the actions and programs of civil authority. Conversely, when the purpose of God is fulfilled through the church, it will have a positive impact on the life and causes of any community. The mission of the church must always transcend any political or national social agenda. Whenever power through political influence becomes either the focus or the means of the church, then the design and purpose of God has been aborted. It is impossible for the freedom, recovery, and release intended by Jesus to occur when political/social criteria are superimposed over the gospel of grace. That is because the healing theme of Jesus is grounded on submission and serving, while the liberation theme of politics is rooted in power and control.

It should also be noted that the meaning of freedom, recovery, and release is not about restoring the body of believers back to what it was before. A companion to the paradigm carried by the

Jews of Jesus's day, that the Messiah would evict Rome, was the belief that He would restore Israel to a religious community that would revolve around the law of Moses and the ritual of the temple. Nothing would be further from His intent, as the law would be replaced with grace and the temple with the church. As he had demonstrated by the parable of wine and wineskins, restoration is about relationships, and freedom is about a new covenant. His followers would not understand the flexible and relevant ministry of the Holy Spirit until after Pentecost. The practical nature of the Spirit is so revolutionary that it continues to be aborted today in favor of the old order of Mosaic law and ritual. The early church attempted to blend the old order of salvation through obedience to the law with the new work of salvation by faith through grace. The result was, and is today, confusion and division, leaving in its wake wounded congregations and unfulfilled believers.

One of the recurring themes of Paul's letters to the churches is the issue of living by faith, never by law. The tendency to adhere to fundamental legalism was so strong that Paul's definition of sin (hamartia) became identified with any kind of adherence to a code or rule. Some of his strongest admonitions are warnings about the loss of grace if there is any hint of legalism.[31] It is evident that the letter to the Galatians was evoked by this primary concern, with a simple, clear argument that adherence to the law brings death, but receiving grace by faith brings life.

The bondages of legalism brought disaster upon the Israelites, and will do the same to the church today. Legalism nullifies the work of Christ on the cross, for it means that salvation is by a means other than Jesus. To place stock in human ability to obey a code has major Christological significance, for it would indicate that Jesus is not adequate, that His work of redemption

---

[31] Galatians 5:4. The emotion Paul feels about the importance of grace instead of law, and the damage done by those who insist on obedience to a code is graphically expressed in 5:12 where he wishes that "they would go the whole way and emasculate themselves!"

was incomplete, and that His sacrifice on our behalf was not fully accepted by God. It also has a disastrous impact on the church, for living by a code denies the ministry of the Holy Spirit and creates barriers to unity. In short, if establishing a rule and a process to enforce it would work, then Jesus didn't have to come and die.

When the community of faith is defined by law (or ritual), hate and fear (instead of love and grace) will always be present with its classification of people, resulting in exclusions and expulsions with inevitable eruptions and explosions in the fellowship. Thus, Paul would state that the church is to be marked by an absence of social discriminations and the presence of mutual love that results in unity: "There is neither Jew nor Greek, slave nor free, male nor female, for you are all one in Christ Jesus" (Galatians 3:28). Whenever there are classes of members, with descending levels of authority and status, that fellowship will be defined by power and control rather than by serving and submission. Prejudice, abuse, and exclusion will afflict the life of that congregation, wrecking its witness in the community as it implodes with spiritual dysfunction and explodes with conflict. Sometimes, in the desire to effect unity, the mistake is often made to attempt uniformity. Uniformity and unity are as different as are law and grace.

These divisive issues often overlap in the church, creating chaos, which wounds both congregations and individuals. However, when they are understood in the context of Jesus's activity and proclamations, it becomes obvious that His agenda was not one of political power, or to replace the Mosaic code with a sacramental or liturgical one, nor to create divisions of people based upon their spirituality. It is a tendency of human nature, perhaps, to systematize the sayings and deeds of Jesus so that we draw those kinds of conclusions and categories of people. But it was the mission of Jesus to create a new people to be His living presence in the world, and not to be just another religious entity.

The mission of Jesus is to bring wholeness to that which was broken, healing to that which was wounded, liberation to that which was in bondage. The words *freedom, recovery,* and *release* are all different forms of healing, including physical. The gospels record many accounts of Jesus affecting physical healing on individuals, even though such healing is a temporary fix. All of the recipients of His healing miracles eventually died. We can conclude that the reason He performed physical healing is to demonstrate the power of God to fix what we cannot repair, so that the bondage of hamartia (sin) could be overcome.

If the goal of Jesus was only physical healing, then why did He single out certain ones, obviously leaving many suffering people in His wake? To suggest that they were left with their physical infirmity as punishment for a weak faith is to suggest that the grace and mercy of God is conditional. A similar crisis arises today when physical healing becomes the focus of faith and an assumed evidence of the presence of God. When someone experiences miraculous healing from a terminal disease, but another person does not, can we conclude that the one healed was more spiritual than the one left suffering? Certainly not! While God cares for our earthly needs, our physical condition is not the primary focus of His design and purpose. Just as wealth is no guarantee of spirituality, good health and unexplained recovery cannot be assumed as evidence of personal spiritual superiority, nor poverty or disease as evidence of a lack of faith.

Why then did Jesus perform physical healing? The answers may vary. There was an overwhelming compassion that motivated Jesus, and some healing events seem to have no other motive than the fact that He was deeply moved by human suffering. In some cases there were obviously other motivations for His healing of certain individuals.[32]

Why did Jesus not heal everyone's physical infirmities? The

---

[32] Galatians 5:4. The emotion Paul feels about the importance of grace instead of law, and the damage done by those who insist on obedience to a code is graphically expressed in 5:12 where he wishes that "they would go the whole way and emasculate themselves!"

answer lies in the motive and message of His healing. His mission was not limited to the nominal needs of humanity, which are locked in time and space dimensions, but more to the deeper phenomenal need of the soul, which is destined for eternity. In that sense it can be said that the reason for every healing event of Jesus's ministry was compassion. Often the individual's physical need was simply a forum for a greater message. By healing people's physical needs, Jesus demonstrated His power over the spiritual powers that wounded humanity. Thus, He posed the question: "Which is easier to say, 'Your sins are forgiven,' or to say, 'Get up and walk'?" Then to drive home the point He answered His own question, "'But so that you may know that the Son of Man has authority on earth to forgive sins' ... Then he said to the paralytic, 'Get up, take your mat and go home' (Matthew 9:5–6).

In the same manner Jesus used the healing of individuals on the Sabbath to reveal the divine superiority of healing over religious codes. In Luke 14, Jesus, on a Sabbath, is confronted with a man suffering from dropsy. Jesus asked the Pharisees and experts in the law, "Is it lawful to heal on the Sabbath or not?" But they remained silent. So taking hold of the man, He healed him and sent him away. Jesus healed because His mission was to fix that which was broken by sin, and that which was broken went deeper than the physical affliction. When He performed a miracle of healing on the Sabbath, it confronted the hypocrisy of the Pharisees. He challenged their hamartia primarily because their legalism was a barrier to their understanding the design and purpose of God to bring healing to the bodies, minds, and souls of humanity.

It was compatible with the oft-repeated warning of the ancient prophets that the Israelites would suffer God's judgment not for their failure to perform religious liturgy but because of their preventing the healing of the real needs of the people. Micah underlines the critical importance: "With what shall I come before the LORD and bow down before the exalted God? Shall I come before him with burnt offerings, with calves a year old? Will the LORD be pleased with thousands of rams, with ten thousand rivers of oil? Shall I offer my firstborn for my transgression, the fruit of my body for the sin of my soul? He has shown you, O man, what is good. And what does the LORD require of you? To act justly and to love mercy and to walk humbly with your God" (Micah 6:6–8).

The root cause of human disaster is sin. We are born with hamartia at work in us. It causes both individuals and the institutions of society to focus on power and possession instead of surrendering to the will of God. Pride, not humbleness, motivates the natural man. Authority and superiority instead of serving and submission dominates and fractures our relationships. Hamartia is so entrenched in our daily lives that without some light in the darkness, violence, abuse, chaos and death continue unchecked. As Paul concludes in Romans 6:23, "the wages of sin is death." It is worth noting that the word translated "wages" is *oywnia* instead of *miskos*. *Miskos* is the common word used in the New Testament for a wage and carries the positive idea of reward. *Oywnia*, on the other hand, brings to mind a very disastrous image of consequence. Both words indicate something that is earned.

In the case of hamartia, what is earned is the unavoidable consequence of death—death of self-esteem, of meaning and purpose, of care and compassion, of relationships, societies, civilizations, and of souls. Death is the consequence of hamartia (sin): missing the mark, having the wrong focus, pursuing the wrong vision, prioritizing the wrong theology. But the gift of God in Christ is to give life, to bring freedom, recovery, and release to the wounded millions through the grace of the cross. His mission is one of healing mercy. It is a mission that is transferred to the church, defining her purpose in the world today.

CHAPTER 10

A New Mandate

Love one another.
—John 13:34

A legitimate question is "What constitutes a successful church?" Is it having more members than the congregation down the street? If we are honest, our American mentality of winners and losers often leads to that conclusion. That is why we hold high the megachurches as evidence of congregational success, when in fact it may be the small, struggling church that is being faithful to God. It is safe to say that churches of all sizes and styles are found to be faithful, and conversely, all kinds of churches are found to be failing. God measures success much differently that we are prone to do. There is an immediate clue that indicates the true spiritual health of a congregation. Whenever a congregation loses its vision and focus (hamartia), the motivation for promotions and programs will often have more to do with numerical additions than growth in Christ. But as most church growth researchers surely know, the only valid numerical growth is a consequence of true spiritual development.

Does success have to do with financial prosperity? This is one of the most common pitfalls of the church. It could be dismissed as a natural fault of the church in a capitalistic society where the bottom line is most important. However, church history indicates that pursuit of wealth has been a stumbling block for the church throughout the centuries. There appears to be an ecclesiastical "Murphy's Law" in that it is the successful businessman who often ends up in control of the church finances so that as in business, the balance sheet dominates the thinking, thus limiting the church's vision. Yes, financial resources are important, but only as a means, not an end. Leith Anderson points out that church and para-church organizations are now part of the world economic system. As a result the ecclesiastical agenda is increasingly being set by economics.[33]

Success in the church is identified by George Barna as its ability to "change people's lives by bringing them into a deeper relationship with God, through faith in Christ and the indwelling power of the Holy Spirit."[34] That is a good definition, especially according to the traditional evangelical theological mind-set. But good as it is, it does not match up to the definition given by Christ. His definition of success is found in His new mandate: "A new command I give you: Love one another. As I have loved you, so you must love one another. By this all men will know that you are my disciples, if you love one another" (John 13:34–35).

The idea of a new command is very challenging. It is also an important model for us to understand the nature of God and the motif of the church. The creative nature of God is expressed in the concept of the word *new*. The divine purpose of the church reflects that creative nature by the emphasis on the *new*. There is much talk these days in some evangelical churches about "revival." When I recently asked a colleague what he meant by "revival," he responded by expressing a longing for a movement of the Spirit of God as in the days of Jonathan Edwards, Charles Finney, and Billy Graham. His response echoed a longing for the "good old days" of the Spirit. While not intended, it may suggest that God

---

[33] Leith Anderson, *A Church for the 21st Century* (Minneapolis: Bethany House, 1992), 27–30.

[34] George Barna, *User Friendly Churches* (Ventura: Regal, 1991), 24.

is tired or is not working or is not as powerful now as He once was in the past. It is a trap of spiritual nostalgia to believe that if we go back to doing things as they were done "back then," we will have the same kind of spiritual awakening they experienced in "the good old days." For the believer, the good days of the Spirit of God are always right now.

The word *revival* does not appear in the Bible. *Revive,* as in "to resuscitate," appears only four times—all Old Testament references. To return to the nostalgic past has never been the way of God. While it is often the natural way of humanity, it has been a barrier to humanity experiencing the good *"now"* days. The Israelites failed to see Jesus for who He was, because of their religious and national nostalgia. They were stuck in the past. They saw their status with God defined by the "good old days" of temple worship, the military might of David's throne, and their singular occupation of the promised land. That nostalgic memory blinded them to the big picture of God's kingdom and his purpose which would be fulfilled in the church.

In contrast to *revival,* the word *new* appears nearly two hundred times in the Bible, with significant emphasis on concepts such as *new heart, new covenant, new people, new way, new teaching, new wine, new wineskins, new command, new creation, new self, new order, new name, new birth, new heaven, new earth, new song,* and so on. In Revelation 21:5 is the final proclamation: "He who was seated on the throne said, 'I am making everything new!'" Obviously, to understand the church in the paradigm of the "old," and as a modern version of ancient Israel, is a critical mistake. In the same way, to return the church to what it was in the past is a mistake. Too many changes are new. Virtually every facet of our world has undergone revolutionary changes (social, cultural, governmental, educational, communal, familial, corporate, etc.). Accordingly, it seems more appropriate that instead of praying for "revival," we should be seeking "renewal."

To suggest the use of "renewal" instead of "revival" is more than semantics. It is a critical awareness of the radical nature of the new covenant. "He saved us, not because of righteous things we had done, but because of his mercy. He saved us through the washing of rebirth and renewal by the Holy Spirit" (Titus 3:5). Renewal is a return, but not to the forms or formulae of the past. It is a return to daily dependency on the Holy Spirit, who always leads God's people into the realm of the "new mandate." Renewal means that the focus is not on the way things were, but on the way things will be. Renewal is always about yielding to the Spirit of God, who takes the open heart and transforms it into a heart for God. Renewal means to trust God, not our habits or our history. Renewal means to respond to all situations from a heart motivated by love.

When Jesus uttered his "new mandate," He was talking to a people who were driven by a commandment-centered paradigm. The original law of Moses had evolved into hundreds of commandments over the years. That drove the lifestyle and expectations of the more religious element, including the Pharisees, to live in compliance with the letter of the law so that they could feel secure in their standing before God. But as Jesus often pointed out, in their failure to fulfill the intent of the law, they had adopted replacement laws that stood in opposition to the nature of God.

In contrast, the apostle Paul, in writing to the church, challenged the habit of reducing the design and purpose of God into a code by exposing the impossibility of living up to the old law. He points out that the unavoidable result of trying to achieve a righteous standing before God through such human effort is guaranteed failure, guilt, and condemnation.

Jesus's use of the word *command* was more than accidental. Knowing of their bent to dependency on the law, He uses the very word they had counted on to introduce a whole new paradigm for being identified as the new people of God. The "new command" is not one of ritual but of lifestyle. The old law could often be performed without impacting the heart and will of the individual. That was especially true regarding the plethora of rules that had evolved from it. They had developed an ability to fulfill the overt behavior required by the rules, while being motivated by desires and purposes which in turn defied the design and purpose of God. Some of the harshest words uttered by Jesus were about the error of such contradiction and were directed at the devoutly legalistic Pharisees. He said they were beautiful on the outside—that is, they appeared to be very pure and holy in their public expressions of religious piety—but inside they were full of all kinds of unclean and unholy pollutants that made them unacceptable to God.[35] The important issue is not about the need for behavioral modification but about transformation of the heart, where the motives that drive behavior are rooted. The new command was not a direction for specific action, but a definition of the heart motive that will radically impact attitude, purpose and behavior.

There is a sense in which Jesus's new mandate was not new. It may have seemed new to his disciples, but it was not new to God. It had been in place since the beginning. Yet, as John writes to the churches, "I am not writing you a new command but an old one, which you have had since the beginning. This old command is the message you have heard" (1 John 2:7–8). It is a new command because, like light, it always penetrates the darkness.

Three parts to the new commandment reveal the ethic of a Christ-transformed heart. First, there is the directive itself: "Love one another." Second, there is the reason for compliance: "As I have loved you, so you must love one another." Third, there is the

---

[35] Matthew 23:27: "Woe to you, teachers of the law and Pharisees, you hypocrites! You are like whitewashed tombs, which look beautiful on the outside but on the inside are full of dead men's bones and everything unclean."

impact that results: "By this all men will know that you are my disciples, if you love one another." It was a significant moment for Jesus and his followers. As Jesus neared the violent end of his earthly mission, he faced a horrific conclusion that would dramatically connect the lostness of humanity with the love of God. In the shadow of the cross, he uttered the *summum bonum* for the church—"love one another." Love—not law or liturgy or laughter—love is the identifying quality and the divine formula for healing that which is broken.

The reason Jesus mandated love is that it reflects the essential nature of God (1 John 4:8, 16). Nothing else that man does reveals the image of God as do the activities of *agape*. Love is the alternative to hamartia. The opposite of love is not just to hate. We are lost when we live by any other motivation than to love. The absence of love leads to the brokenness of humanity, and conversely, it is the exercise of love that brings redemption, restoration, and renewal. Actually, Jesus's new command should not have seemed so new to the disciples. He had said it in other ways before. But that is the way of hamartia—we are so intently focusing on the wrong mark that we do not hear the words of healing and renewal.

On one occasion the religious experts asked Jesus, "What is the greatest commandment of all?" Jesus's response was consistent as he expounded on the law of love: "'Love the Lord your God with all your heart and with all your soul and with all your mind. This is the first and greatest commandment.' And the second is like it, 'Love your neighbor as yourself.' All the Law and the Prophets hang on these two commandments" (Matt. 22:34–40). It is impossible to understand God apart from His actions of love, and it is impossible to love God without extending that same kind of love to others. Jesus alone became the evidence of what that kind of love means. Too often love has been filtered through a doctrinal position, such as election, thereby limiting its scope. Others screen love by a theological mentor's perspective, such as a John Calvin or John

Wesley.[36] While such spiritual giants speak truth, the danger of making their interpretation a litmus test for orthodoxy is that it can lead to nonloving actions, such as criticism, accusation, and religious cleansing of the church. When people become the victims of doctrinal wars, the one sure conclusion is that love is set aside. While knowing truth that is rooted in biblical orthodoxy is very important, to use it to exclude or reject others is unacceptable. Such reactions have no place in *agape*.

Any model or theology of love that has as its focus anyone or anything other than Jesus Christ is in error. Sadly, it is an error that continues to contribute to the wounding of individuals and fellowships. The only model of love that will bring about healing is one that seeks to prioritize what Jesus prioritized, to exercise what he exercised, and to act in concert with the same Spirit who empowered his sacrifice of love. Those who would be known as Christians have only one criterion for theological excellence: to love others in the same way that Christ loves all men. A Spirit-filled congregation is one that is marked by love. It is that essential quality that brings healing to those who enter therein, and enables it to be a place of healing instead of wounding.

The arguments for maintaining a high standard of orthodoxy for those who would become part of the church are numerous and must be seriously considered. Given the pluralism of contemporary society in a culture that is very spiritualized, but not holy, knowing truth from error is increasingly important. The moral and ethical issues dividing our nation today are nothing new, except they are given more urgency because of the power of technology. However, they are being used as battering rams on the church door, threatening to create divisions more severe than any

---

[36] Mildred Wynkoop, *A Theology of Love* (Kansas City: Beacon Hill Press, 1972). This is an expose of Wesleyan theology. Her "Implications of a Theology of Love," pp. 27–31, is a worthy review of the subject. Unfortunately, Wynkoop uses Wesleyan theology as the standard to argue with John Calvin's theology, confusing the idea of love.

of the doctrinal cleavages of the past. The importance of orthodox theology has never been more critical to being able to discern truth from error. It seems that the proponents of alternative moral standards for believers, standards that line up with the relativistic values of naturalism instead of the holiness standards of theistic faith, have also abandoned biblical orthodoxy. The bastion of "faithfulness" is often collapsing under the rubric of "relevancy," which is nothing more than compromise. The danger for those in the church who detect the erosion of biblical truth within the church is that they will react with a "theological cleansing" that will destroy many and send others off into spiritual refugee camps. It is critical that, in our renewed emphasis on biblical truth, the highest form of theological and doctrinal orthodoxy be kept at the top, which is to love. It will do no good to be theologically right if we allow ourselves to react to the wrongs of society with wrong religion. We do well to remember Paul's admonition, "For in Christ Jesus neither circumcision nor uncircumcision (read "theological orthodoxy") has any value. The only thing that counts is faith expressing itself through love" (Galatians 5:6).

Jesus's new mandate to love is uniquely designed for the church. It does not simply replace the law but is the practical application of all God intended by it. In that sense it supersedes both law and doctrine in that love reduces them down to a mundane reality. The only way to fulfill the law is to exercise love, and the only way to explain doctrine is to respond to all situations with love. It is a serious paradigm shift (see chapter 12) that impacts what we do with people who have wrong or inadequate beliefs, whose lifestyles are less than holy, and who desire to be part of the body of Christ, even though they don't measure up. Love does impact how we respond to the issues of sexual orientation and abortion and the coming issues of euthanasia, fetal-tissue research, and cloning, along with many unseen challenges to our sense of "rightness and purity." Until a church gets the "new mandate" into first place in their list of important orthodoxy, grace, truth, and mercy will never become a reality. But when love is the standard by which we evangelize, disciple, worship, and serve, then that fellowship experiences a dynamic of the Spirit that is healing, renewing, and profoundly transforming.

CHAPTER 11

Roots

From his roots a Branch will bear fruit.
—Isaiah 11:1

Mary and Lester lived on Guemes Island near Anacortes, north of Seattle. Both Lester, a retired research doctor from University of Washington Medical Center, and Mary, a retired nurse, came to Christ late in life. In the mornings they would arise and look to the east over Padilla Bay to Mount Baker. Across the road on the other side of their home was Lester's large workshop and Mary's abundant vegetable garden with its high fence designed to keep the deer out. She was an avid and accomplished gardener, and any visitor during the growing season left with a supply of fresh vegetables. Among her favorite possessions was an impressive collection of bonsai trees.

Bonsai are not small species that look like real trees. They are miniature versions of the real thing. Some of her bonsai trees were miniature versions of the same large trees in the forest around their house. One could stand and look at the large, natural version of a tree looming a hundred feet high and then glance down to observe Mary's bonsai version that is only about two feet tall and little more than three or four inches in diameter. The visible difference between the two plants is size. That translates into a difference of function. The large fir tree is a good windbreak and shade tree, and if harvested, the large tree will produce several thousand board feet of lumber, enough to build a house.

In contrast, the small bonsai tree, beyond providing pleasure to a gardener, is good for decorative purposes and a conversation piece. However, the significant difference between the two versions of the tree lies beneath the surface. What determines the size is the root system of each tree. The bonsai tree is small because Mary clips the roots and keeps them small—small roots, small tree. Some of her trees are very old but remain small because their roots are never allowed to grow.[37]

The bonsai provides a meaningful spiritual metaphor that can apply equally to one's private life or to the life of a local congregation. Whether it's trees or churches, the size and purpose of the visible part is directly related to and dependent upon the size of the root system. The root system, that which provides foundational support and resource, although not glamorous or seen, is critical to that which is visible and functional.

This is the point of the parable Jesus told about the sower and what happens to the seed on different kinds of soils. It is one of His parables found in all three of the synoptic gospels. Some seed fell on a path and was picked off by birds. Other seed fell on rocky soil and, after a good start, withered and died. Some fell on thorny soil, and as it grew, it was choked out by the weeds. And some fell on good soil and produced an abundant crop. At first reading it appears that the problem is the soil that keeps the plant from maturing and producing. But after hearing Jesus's interpretation, we discover that the real issue is what happens to the plant that keeps it from becoming productive. Jesus points out the three most consistent causes of spiritual death. Each applies equally to individuals and to congregations.

The first is unbelief, a loss of confidence in the truth of

---

[37] Lester passed away a few years ago. Mary continues to care for her bonsai trees, along with maintaining her wonderful gardens.

God. For many churches the impact of modernism, with its deconstruction of scripture, denial of the deity of Christ, rejection of miracles, and abandonment of a doctrine of salvation, has had disastrous results. The second cause of spiritual decline is failure to develop an adequate root system. The rocky ground, where there is not very much soil for the plant to take root, is indicative of those "who, since they have no root, last only a short time. When trouble or persecution comes because of the word, they quickly fall away" (Luke 8:13). The third spiritual dysfunction is that of lack of focus, of missing the mark (hamartia). The cares and issues of life dominate and the priorities of the kingdom of God are never developed or nurtured.

While the point of the parable is to describe the common causes of personal spiritual dysfunction (unbelief, shallowness, and busy-ness) compared to those "who hear the word, retain it, and by persevering produce a crop" (Luke 8:15), it is also intended as a message for the church. The church is made up of a people who are rooted and grounded in Christ so that as a community they *produce a crop*. The size of their root system— the largeness or the smallness of their relationship to Christ, the dependency of the congregation on the work of Christ by faith, and their commitment to His mandate to love unconditionally— will determine the spiritual harvest of the congregation. God measures the success of a congregation differently than does the world, and a "mega" church in His eyes has nothing to do with the number of people in attendance but has everything to do with the prayers that seek His will, the adherence to His inspired word, and the level of surrender to the purpose and will of Christ.

The apostle Paul applies the same imagery in the eleventh chapter of Romans with the critical importance of the church, like her spiritual predecessor, Israel, being rooted in the holiness of God: "If the root is holy, so are the branches" (Rom. 11:16). In that same passage he underlines the dependency of the branch (church) on the root (Christ): "You do not support the root, but the root supports you" (Rom. 11:18). It is a critical spiritual reality that impacts all aspects of life for the authentic follower of Christ.

In the same way, and with the same critical importance, it is also deeply relevant to what goes on in a local congregation. Bonsai congregations have limited root systems. They get their clues for ministry, worship style, and fellowship ideas from somewhere other than the Word of God. Their mandates for faith and practice are more a reaction to the culture around them than a response to the will of God discovered through the inspired word and the infilling Holy Spirit. Bonsai congregations may look nice, attractive, and unique, and they may be good conversation pieces, but they produce little or no spiritual fruit. Their witness, if there is any, remains very small; their influence in people's lives and in the community is minimal. Bonsai churches are good only for people's religious hobby interest and for conversational topics at gatherings. In the words of Jesus in Matthew 7:16, "By their fruit you will recognize them. Do people pick grapes from thorn bushes, or figs from thistles?"

However, a small root system is not the only problem that afflicts the church and results in low productivity and high conflict. Bonsai churches may not experience open conflict. Their style is more of an *implosion* than of an *explosion* experience. Churches that explode into open warfare and division, leaving souls scattered across the congregational battlefields often suffer from a different root problem. Shallowness, rather than smallness, often describes their root system.

Before I began my pastoral journey, I worked as a timber faller in the Blue Mountains of Oregon. In those days it was a respected, if not an honorable, occupation. In terms of the span of my life, it lasted only a few years, but it provided many experiences and lessons that continue to impact me today. Those were the days before the issue of spotted owl habitat was used by the government to stop the harvest of timber. However, other environmental concerns were already impacting the logging industry. For example, we were required to practice selective logging. Only "ripe" trees were harvested, which meant that in a grove of pines, some tall, beautiful, large trees were left standing as future seed trees. It was assumed that the removal of older and mature trees would allow the remaining trees to grow larger more quickly.

The first time I walked back through one of those thinned-out groves after a wind storm, I was surprised to find strong, healthy trees lying on the ground with their huge root system sticking into the air. Those same trees had obviously withstood more violent storms in the past. But this time they had been toppled by the wind. The reason they did not stand was their huge but shallow root system. In the past they had been protected by the larger, deeper rooted trees before loggers removed them. Instead of growing a deep root system down through the soil to anchor into the mountain, the remaining trees left by the loggers had developed a large, but shallow, root system that spread out just under the surface. Shallow roots, while they may be large and effective in gathering nutrients for growth, are ineffective in standing against the storms that inevitably come.

Just as storms that test a tree's root system are certain in the mountains, storms that test churches are likewise certain to come along. Hardship, difficulties, challenges, and controversial issues are normal for a spiritually viable fellowship. They are the stuff of life in the world that provide opportunities for healthy ministry design that is relevant to the community around the church. The fact that a congregation experiences difficulty may be an indication that the enemy is losing territory and is therefore bringing pressure in hopes that conflict will diminish spiritual effectiveness. Challenges are an important element in a church that has a healthy root system. It is both naive and foolish to think a healthy church is one without challenges or struggles. However, while difficulty is normal, conflict and division are not. The difference is found in the roots. Jesus said that the tragedy of some is that they are excited for the kingdom but they do not survive because they have no root (Matt. 13:3–23). Our usual ego-centered paradigm of Jesus's teachings leads us to interpret that parable as having to do with individual salvation. It is worth noting that it is one of a series of kingdom parables. The message is really about the kingdom (i.e., the nature of the church).

Unlike bonsai churches that have a small root system, shallow congregations are often large, complex, and progressive fellowships. They may have a large physical plant and multiple staff persons representing a variety of ministries. But they also may be spread out so far, with so many programs and ministries, that they fail to put down deep roots anchored into the essentials of faith. It is extremely easy to convince oneself that whatever is urgent or popular or is "bringing in" more attendees is also essential! The most important elements of a healthy and productive congregation will be discussed later in this book. The evidence of the need to reevaluate priorities and check out the anchor points of a church is exposed when storms arise. If the root system of a congregation is shallow, that is, if it is dependent on such things as money, facility, denominational loyalty, eschatological positions, worship styles, more people than the church next door, and so on, and is not anchored to the fundamental elements of the Rock (surrender to the Spirit, seeking God's will in prayer, trusting in His sovereign way, being dependent on grace in Christ, and exercising unconditional love, to name a few), then storms will often bring with them conflict, division, and disaster.

Testing is essential for spiritual growth and maturity. Jesus said in John 16:33, "I have told you these things, so that in me you may have peace. In this world you will have trouble. But take heart! I have overcome the world." James, the elder statesman of the early church who had witnessed the challenges and deadly persecution that the first citizens of the Way experienced, writes with spiritual insight: "Consider it pure joy, my brothers, whenever you face trials of many kinds, because you know that the testing of your faith develops perseverance. Perseverance must finish its work so that you may be mature and complete, not lacking anything" (James 1:2–4). He understood that church life is of necessity a series of storms (issues and trends) that impact and stress the church. If a church is shallow-rooted, it may succumb to the storms, either by capitulating to the world so that the church loses its distinctive ability to be the light in darkness or by falling into internal conflict and division, being uprooted and unable to minister God's grace to a desperate world.

Challenges and debate are fuel for a fired-up, healthy congregation. But conflict and division are always symptoms of spiritual pathology, a sickness of the soul of the congregation. Jesus designed his church to exist in unity. Conflict and division expose a root problem. Therefore, when a church experiences conflict and becomes divided, it not only is compromised in its ability to be God's vessel of grace to that community, but also it is in need of help. Again, it must be underlined that differences and diversity are important and must not be perceived as conflict and division. Unity does not mean uniformity, and debate is healthy and important in avoiding conflict. However, when conflict becomes a persistent experience and removes the Spirit from a congregation, then finding ways back to healthy debate and acceptable diversity will involve a rediscovery of the divine roots upon *whom* the church stands.

What are the strong roots for a healthy and healing church? At the risk of mixing metaphors, we must discern the subtle but essential difference between roots and foundations. Foundations give form and style to a church in the same way a foundation for a house provides the shape and security for what is built. In the church there are several critical foundational elements upon which a healthy and holy congregation builds its ministry form. They include prayer (*proseuchomai*), which is to cry out to God; teaching (*didasko*), which has to do with instructing in the truth; worship (*proskeuneo*), which is akin to praying and is to focus on God in surrender and praise; and fellowship (*koinonia*), which reflects the essential nature the community of believers have in being the living presence of Christ. There are a number of excellent books available that expand on these and other foundational functions of the church. My purpose here is not to evaluate how these foundational exercises of the healing church are to be carried out, but to point out the difference between the foundational functions and the essential roots on which those functions rest.

To continue the mixed metaphor, roots are like the footings upon which the foundation stands. Footings spread out and fit the contour of the ground, giving a deeper, wider and more intimate footprint for the building that will emerge from the foundation. The foundation, like theological truths, is poured within forms that determine its shape and height. While the foundation gives shape to a building, unless it is placed on a solid footing, it will eventually settle, resulting in a defective, and maybe even a dangerous, building. That is what we witness in churches that have emphasized one or more of the foundational functions while neglecting the footing (roots).

Take for example the current division in so many churches over worship style. True worship is rooted in love—love of God and love of the brethren. Love, one of the ultimate definitions of God, was a root issue for Jesus. Worship without love ignores other people's needs while insisting on your own preferences. When we demand our own way in worship at the expense of everyone else, it is not holy, God-focused worship. It is hamartia, the sin of focusing on self, ultimately the idolatry of self. The result is division instead of unity, and wounding instead of healing other seekers.

The same kind of scenario can be found with all the other important foundational elements of the church. There are many calls for people to pray today. Prayer is a foundational issue, and there are powerful testimonies of what can happen when a congregation gets on their collective knees. Brooklyn, New York, pastor Jim Cymbala's books *Fresh Wind, Fresh Fire; Fresh Faith;*

and *Fresh Power* provide inspiring examples of the positive impact of prayer. But unless prayer is rooted in surrender to God, by a heart that is submitting to His ways and means and exercising faith and trust in His sovereign will, our prayers are little more than self-seeking petitions. It is not good enough for a church to combat the literacy issue in the church with an outstanding Bible teaching ministry if love, truth, and mercy are not the roots upon which all biblical truth is grounded.

What are the essential roots that support, nurture, and bond together all that comprises the healthy, holy, and healing church? There are four that seem to be essential in every aspect of the Way, whether it be theological foundations, fellowship functions, or organizational formats: *love, truth, grace,* and *mercy.* These qualities of God are the lifeblood that must flow through every aspect of the fellowship. Leave one out of the mix, and it becomes a mess. Truth without love or grace or mercy becomes a harsh and cruel tyrant. Grace without truth, mercy, and love condones sin. Too often it seems that these essential roots for the church are relegated to doctrines or theologies, almost as if it is a choice whether or not to incorporate them into one's religious belief system. When analyzing what is at the root of a conflicted congregation, or a troubled marriage, or broken relationships of any kind, it becomes evident that one or more of these root sources has been restricted or rejected. Therefore, it is essential for any congregation, marriage, or relationship in the name of God to carefully consider and incorporate into all aspects of life each of these essential footings.

CHAPTER 12

Love

The greatest of these is love.
—1 Corinthians 13:13

The church emerged during times of great social, political, and religious stress. Sometimes the believers of the Way were simply victims of adverse events that took place, and other times they were the specific target of persecution. Either way, it often meant that early Christians were often displaced into unusual surroundings and strange cultures. Most of the early believers were Jewish, which meant they already had a cultural orientation to life wherever they landed. As Jews, even in a foreign land, they were cloistered together and their heritage and religion combined to define their values, ethics and social relationships. However, it soon became evident that embracing Christ meant they often were not welcomed into the Jewish community. More importantly, their new faith brought with it a different ethic, one that revolved around a simple but profound principle called *love*. It was an ethic that transcended cultural boundaries and created a new people who existed in healthy relationships with people of any culture.

To support and encourage these early believers, letters of guidance and encouragement were written by the apostles to believers scattered among the various cultures of the first-century church. As those writings were assimilated into what would become the Holy Bible, it became evident that several common themes ran through these early writings, which provided evidence that the writers were inspired by the same Holy Spirit. The most common and important theme is love, particularly that form of love modeled and taught by Christ. In the letters of Paul, *agape* love became the hallmark of authentic faith and the essential function of personal spiritual renewal. In his letters, Paul not only repeated the mandate "to love," he provided a rationale that revealed the divine wisdom of the *Great Commandment*. Three primary texts underlined the critical element of love to the church and exposed what is usually missing when controversy leads to a conflicted congregation.

1 Corinthians 13

One of the best-known chapters of the Bible, both in and out of the church, is Paul's treatise on *love* in 1 Corinthians 13. He was writing to correct the social, moral, and spiritual abuses that damage individuals and bring conflict to congregations. The Corinthian church was a place of constant conflict, an unacceptable condition that Paul sought to correct. He began by describing the nature of true believers as redeemed and forgiven people who exercise *love*. Up front, he expresses the idea that if one does not have Christ-like love, nothing else matters. In his opening (vv. 1–3), he touches on some of the most cherished evidences of godliness in the church: eloquent preaching, insight into prophecy, scriptural knowledge, effective faith, denial of worldly goods for the sake of others, and martyrdom. It is a list of some of the highest standards believers in every century have held up as evidence of sainthood.

We revere those individuals who are gifted in preaching by hanging on their every word. If they also exhibit insights into the mysteries of prophetic texts, they can build huge followings. Perhaps it is more so now than in the early church, but we also hold high the reading and memorizing of scripture and the knowledge of doctrine as evidence of being very spiritual. Of course, the person who often models our highest ideal of being spiritual is the one who rejects personal fame and fortune and goes to a mission field to share the gospel. But for Paul, it was nothing but noise, a waste of time and energy if the gifted, learned, or sacrificing individual did not have *love*. Unless it is motivated by *agape* love, it counts for nothing.

What is *agape*? As if reading the reactionary-minded generations of readers, in the second section (vv. 4–8a) Paul provided a list of the qualities of *love*, couched in human-character terms, describing the way God loves and how Christ loves us, and as such Paul's list became a list of the qualities that characterize congregations who are fulfilling Jesus's new mandate to "love as I have loved you."

The intimate human qualities of *love* used here stand in stark contradiction to how it sometimes appears in the church. When *agape* is discussed in the context of the church, it often appears to take on the sheen of a theological conversation in which we use sterile and nonpersonal concepts that have little to do with reality. The characteristics of *love* stated here are significant, for they establish the practical criteria for the new mandate. Each is worth meditating on, for they are the essential values in the theology of healing wounded congregations.

There are sixteen qualities in all. Eight of them are strong negatives, describing what is *not* of *agape*—what is absent in God's nature and in Christ's life. They are qualities missing because they are the essence of hamartia, the sin of acting with wrong priorities. As such, they are the cause of the brokenness that troubles our world, including the conflicted church. The wrongness of the behavior in each case is indicated by the negative adverb "*not*." It emphasizes permanency in that these activities, attitudes and behaviors are *never* actions of *agape love*.

According to Paul in 1 Corinthians 13, love

- does not envy;
- does not boast;
- is not proud;
- is not rude;
- is not self-seeking;
- is not easily angered;
- keeps no record of wrongs; and
- does not delight in evil.

Each of the above destructive and non-love traits demand that the reader stop and consider their implication. They are not of love because they radiate out from a heart that has self at the center. It is safe to say that in every wounded member and in every dysfunctional congregation, at least one of the negative qualities listed above is dominant. In most cases there are multiples of the above negative qualities at work at the same time. They are the elements of broken relationships in personal lives, as well as in damaged and divided congregations. Typically, in conflicted churches, these *nots* have engulfed both pastor and people so subtly and completely that convictions of "being in the right" are held even to the point of destroying the fellowship. How radically opposite such thinking is from the *love* Christ demonstrated in His work of redemption. How far removed it is from His passionate prayer for the unity of His followers.

The other eight characteristics of *agape* are descriptions of the heart of God and, as such, a listing of the way Christ loves. They also describe the qualities of character that identify the Christ-centered heart of people who have truly experienced the impact of grace. It is the ultimate inside-out experience. The experience of receiving a new heart upon repentance and confession of faith in Christ demands that the non-love characteristics and negative habits listed above are replaced with the positive, Christ-like activities of *agape*. It is unreasonable to think that a Christ-centered heart will produce the non-love behaviors and attitudes listed above. Likewise, it is foolish to think that a self-centered heart can produce the positive, godly qualities listed below. What follows are more than behavioral forms but constitute the essential qualities that mark individuals and congregations who are known as disciples of Jesus. Just as the presence of the negative traits in any form destroys people and churches, the presence of *love* as a driving force in believers will bring healing and life to people and to congregations. The following characteristics are qualities of *agape* that identify the people of God:

Paul, in 1 Corinthians 13, says that love

- is patient;
- is kind;
- rejoices with the truth;
- always protects;
- always trusts;
- always hopes;
- always perseveres; and
- never fails.

Again it is important for the reader to contemplate the impact of each word. It is interesting to note the strong descriptive words that accompany some of the characteristics of love in the above lists. "Always" and "never" reveal the absolute and positive nature of the love of God. They are reminders of the unconditional love that sent the Savior to Calvary, and a challenge to all believers to develop that same kind of absolute, unconditional *love*, and practice it in the fellowship of believers.

Here is the genius of the true church, for when these qualities of *patience, kindness, truth, protection, trust, hope, perseverance,* and *faithfulness* are proactive in the individuals who make up a fellowship, then the grace of God in Christ becomes a living reality. Like nothing else in all the world, no other organization, cause, or power, the healing of the wounded heart is accomplished through love. Amazingly, not only is the deep wound of sin brought to wholeness through *love*, but also the transformation of a life takes place as the focus on oneself is replaced by a desire to know and to do God's will.

The third section (8b–12) points out the reason why a focus on the activities of faith apart from *love* always fails. In this life we are limited in our reasoning powers, our abilities to see the future, and our abilities to accomplish. In the same way that an immature child is incapable of understanding the reasons for a parent's directives, we are incapable of comprehending the ways of God. The only way we can implement the nature and wisdom of God into our lives is to exercise *love*. So Paul concludes this foundational truth with the extraordinary statement that *love* is greater than either faith or hope.

At first this seems unacceptable, for it is by faith we are saved, and it is hope that drives our pursuit of God. But when we comprehend that faith absent love is merely wishful thinking, and hope without love is a fantasy land, then the statement becomes not only true but also reveals the first-things-first standard for a successful church: "And now these three remain: faith, hope, and love. But the greatest of these is love" (v.13).

Galatians 5

A warning is necessary at this point. The replacement of the law[38] with the single mandate to *love* could be interpreted as an end of God's call to be a holy people. Some, choosing to misinterpret grace in a permissive manner, have used the idea of *love* to excuse

---

[38] The death of the law was a critical point of Paul's theology of grace. In Col. 2:14 he describes the written code as having been "canceled ... with its regulations, that was against us and that stood opposed to us; he took it away, nailing it to the cross."

an ungodly lifestyle, which is an abuse of the intent of the mandate. The result is not only moral sin but chaos that damages the self, other people, societies, cultures, and the church. In reaction to such abuse, there is a powerful temptation to adopt a substitute code to replace the law of love. Invariably, the dominant alternative is to return to some form of the Mosaic law, or derivatives thereof. It is a hamartia of the worst kind.

Paul uses strong language to point out the disaster of any hint of legalism. Any form of the law, whether it be an implied or required ritual, denies the grace of God and, as such, rejects Christ.[39] The result is soul death, for in rejecting the grace of God in Christ, it rejects the way of salvation. Not only that but also any code that supplants love sets up the believer in an impossible dilemma, for the very nature of the law is impossible to fulfill. The only reason for the law was to prepare the way (expose the need) for love—incarnated love. To seek to live by a code lands one in the worst kind of bondage, from which there is no escape except through Christ. The problem for those who need some kind of rule of law in order to feel holy is that to accept Christ as Savior and Lord is to absolutely reject any hint of law. Perhaps worst of all, the intrusion of legalism into the fellowship of *love* brings division and bondage, destroying the unity of the fellowship.

In Ephesians, Paul points out that when the unity of the fellowship is broken, the image of God to the world is distorted, and the light that dispels darkness is reduced to a flicker. The laws of hamartia erect walls of prejudice that result in hostility, division, absence of joy, and religious bondage. In contrast, the love of Christ knocks down the walls of division. Jesus always liberates: "It is for freedom that Christ has set us free" (Galatians 5:1).

Paul reduces all religious practice down to the basic root

---

[39] Gal. 5:1–2: "It is for freedom that Christ has set us free. Stand firm, then, and do not let yourselves be burdened again by a yoke of slavery. Mark my words! I, Paul, tell you that if you let yourselves be circumcised, Christ will be of no value to you at all."

of *love*: "The only thing that counts is faith expressing itself through love" (Galatians 5:6). The reason for his confidence in the power of *love* to result in a higher moral lifestyle is that when love is exercised, the standards of morality are elevated. In the image of Jesus, to love another person is to never do anything that will hurt that person or cause harm to him or her. Instead, it is to do what will bring healing, wholeness, joy, and completeness in their life.

When love dominates a congregation, the members seek what is best for one another: "Do not use your freedom to indulge the sinful nature; rather, serve one another in love" (Galatians 5:13). Immorality and resulting conflict strikes when individuals serve self: "So I say, live by the Spirit, and you will not gratify the desires of the sinful nature" (Galatians 5:16). The reason for this is simple yet eternal. Any fellowship under the influence of the Holy Spirit will be characterized by these qualities, "love, joy, peace, patience, kindness, goodness, faithfulness, gentleness and self-control" (Galatians 5:22–23). *Love* being placed first in that list is no accident. As was pointed out in the 1 Corinthians section, without the driving motivation of *love*, none of the rest will matter. Most likely, without *love* most of the rest will not happen. Love fulfills the law.

Ephesians 4

In his letter to the Ephesians, Paul continues to emphasize the relationship of love and unity. He commends the unity that has characterized the church at Ephesus. After affirming the nature of the church and the standing of the believer in Christ, he challenges the Ephesians to live close to Christ for the sake of unity. Chapter 4 begins with a reminder that all followers of Christ are called to live in the image of the Lord, which results in a peaceful unity: "I urge you to live a life worthy of the calling you have received. Be completely humble and gentle; be patient, bearing with one another in love. Make every effort to keep the unity of the Spirit through the bond of peace" (Ephesians 4:1–3).

The repeat of some of the Corinthian qualities of love is not incidental. The ability of any congregation to avoid conflict and experience a peaceful unity is dependent on the intentional effort of the individuals in that fellowship to exercise the characteristics of *love*. That reaches crescendo in chapter 5 as he begins with the familiar charge to all who would be known as Christians: "Be imitators of God, therefore, as dearly loved children and live a life of love, just as Christ loved us and gave himself up for us as a fragrant offering and sacrifice to God" (5:1–2).

Paul then goes on to make application of that principle of *agape* to the primary relationships of life whether in personal motives, in marriage relationships, in the home, or at work. It is in these primary relationships that living by the rule of *love* has its greatest impact on the entire community. He concludes by stating that he is talking about Christ and the church. It is an interchangeable condition. If one loves Christ in the church, then one will love God in the private realm of one's personal life and will exercise the qualities of *agape* to one's mate, children, parents, leaders, and fellow workers.

It is worth noting that in Ephesians, Paul uses the word *submit* to capture the essence of love in action, a word that reflects the cross of Christ. In Ephesians 5:21, he predicates the nature of love in unity with "submit to one another out of reverence to Christ." The idea of submission is not well received in contemporary society, or in the church for that matter.[40] But, in the fellowship of believers, the way of Christ is to submit instead of to control. Richards and Hoeldtke noted that in their work on leadership in the church where they point out that there is no place in the church for a paradigm that puts leadership in the position of authority and

---

[40] Church growth leaders often point out that certain concepts and words or traditional Christianity are not part of the Boomer generation, words such as commitment, submission, and obligation.

control.[41] Instead, the quality of leadership most like Christ is that of a servant, one who seeks to respond in a sacrificial way to the needs, wounds, fears, and crises of others.

The greatest example of that servant love is Christ on the cross. As we see Him in the cruel injustice of His death His words echo in our hearts, "Love as I have loved you." The ability of individuals in a congregation to love as he loved becomes a powerful force that transforms the local church from a battle zone into a hospital for the wounded. Submission is the key to loving, and love is the root source for healing wounded churches.

---

[41] Lawrence O. Richards and Clyde Hoeldtke, *A Theology of Church Leadership* (Grand Rapids: Zondervan, 1981), 15–27.

CHAPTER 13

Truth

Surely you desire truth in the inner parts; you
teach me wisdom in the inmost place.
—Psalm 51:6

"What is truth?" Pilate's question (John 18:38) has ricocheted down through the centuries, too often reverberating with conflict and bloody wars in the name of God. It was in that brief conversation at his trial before Pilate that Jesus confessed His mission as one of truth. Breaking the silence that had marked his ordeal, Jesus expands on the question: "In fact, for this reason I was born, and for this I came into the world, to testify to the truth. Everyone on the side of truth listens to me" (John 18:37). Truth was a central theme of Jesus's ministry, it is a fundamental characteristic of God, and it is an essential root for every aspect of the ekklesia, the *body of Christ.* The Greek word is used instead of our English "church" to underline the fact that there is a significant difference between the ekklesia established by Christ and that which has evolved into the "church" today. Ekklesia is deeply rooted in truth; "church" has too often been marked by compromise and convenience.

Truth is foundational to the gospel and to everything that emerges from it. Rather than describe the events or the times surrounding the birth of the Savior, John began his narrative with the revelation that the Messiah was the living incarnation of truth: "The Word became flesh and made his dwelling among us. We have seen his glory, the glory of the One and Only, who came from the Father, full of grace and truth" (John 1:14). Twenty-eight times John's gospel recorded Jesus saying, "I tell you the truth." It was a statement rooted in the eternal fact that He is the living truth. Jesus agreed with John's assessment when he said to Mary, who was grieving over the death of her brother, "I am the way and the truth and the life" (John 14:6). "I am the truth" is significantly different from "I tell you the truth." It indicated a new understanding for truth in the kingdom of grace in comparison to what it had become in the kingdom of the law. The new Israel, the ekklesia (body of Christ), would live by a radically new perception of "truth."

In the old covenant, truth was contained in a law, that was written into a code. It contained rules, regulations, ritual and responsibilities to live by as well as repercussions for violations. Truth, under the law, was a legal document in which God was the policeman, prosecutor, judge, and jury. Plain and simple, one either kept the law or violated it. In the new covenant, truth becomes a radically different paradigm. It is not a new rule or religion but an entirely new way to see, think, and believe. Instead of being constrained by law, truth for the ekklesia is embodied in a person, the living Christ. Instead of being enforced by a code with regulations, truth in the church is celebrated through a relationship that is empowered by love. Instead of being a controlling power that limits life's experiences, the living truth is a spiritual liberator who invites us to experience the fullness of God's creative reality. To the Samaritan woman at the well, Jesus said that "God is spirit" who must be worshiped "in spirit and in truth" (John 4:24).

Worship is different from obedience. One can obey the truth of the law but never truly worship God. Coming to see the incarnate living Christ as the complete essence of truth requires a major shift of one's entire sense of religious rightness. If salvation could be wrought by obedience to the law, then Jesus did not have to come and die. That is the argument Paul made in his letter to the Galatians. His reasoning was that if the law could have brought about the kingdom of God, then Jesus did not have to come: "If a law had been given that could impart life, then righteousness would certainly have come by the law" (Galatians 3:21). He went on to point out that when there is conflict, "biting and devouring one another" in the fellowship of believers, it is because the law has displaced faith in Christ. For wherever faith in Christ is the focus, then love and care for one another will be the result. Conflict is never the result of the Holy Spirit at work through love. But the opposite is true: where there is conflict, it reveals that the spirit of the law has been inserted by "agitators" (Galatians 5:12). He concluded that part of his letter with a clear statement of the difference: "But if you are led by the Spirit, you are not under law" (Galatians 5:18).

To put it into a truth formula, if the law was the ultimate truth, then the incarnation of Jesus Christ was unnecessary. To use the words of Jesus, "I tell you the truth," the truth that is real is not a code or a body of information; it is not a theology or even scientific fact. Truth that is foundational, absolute, ultimate, and eternal is none other than the living God fully revealed in Jesus Christ. Codes, written revelation, theology, and empirical truth are true only to the degree that they reflect the reality of the living Christ.

This truth has major ramifications for the ekklesia and radically impacts the ways and means of a local congregation. At the risk of being criticized by my own congregation and extended fellowship, to say we Baptists are a people of the Bible is not good enough. A Baptist distinctive that we fall back on is that "the Bible is our rule for faith and practice." In a recent document developed for our churches in the Northwest Region of American Baptist

Churches, that biblical foundation is underlined by a commonly held essential of the "authority of scripture."[42]

That is well and good, and certainly better than having Hollywood or the Supreme Court as the determining factors for life in the church. But it is not good enough. Far too often that "Word of God" is used as a club to beat each other's religious brains out instead of as a vessel to lead us to the living truth. How many churches have experienced conflict and even have divided over the Bible, whether it be what translation to read, the hermeneutic used, or the interpretation of certain passages? The number is staggering.

Jesus's prayer for the unity of his followers as they experience and practice the gifts of the Spirit is set aside in such abuse of others over the recorded truth. How many people have suffered criticism and experienced condemnation by people who use the Bible as a ways and means to judge others? It is horrifying to realize that the message of reconciliation and the cross of grace is used as a tool for division and abuse. At the root of such chaos and division is a hamartia of the Bible or of certain passages. This kind of error happens when the idea of truth is something in written form instead of the living person of Jesus Christ.

Truth is a root issue because it is experienced not memorized. Truth is not discovered by knowing facts, however true they may be, but in knowing and trusting God. While the law was good, it was limited by the code that gave it power. The original intent was to bless the Israelites by guiding them to a place of reliance, trust, and hope in the living God. The same is true for God's people today. While the Bible is an incredible resource for experiencing the truth, an inspired and holy revelation of the nature and purposes of God, its greatest value is its unique ability to reveal Christ and then to help believers to walk by the Spirit in reliance and hope in the living God. This relationship with the living God

---

[42] American Baptist Churches of the Northwest *Vision Statement* (2002).

flows through every aspect of our lives and needs to format all the decisions, ministries, relationships, and activities of a church. It is a root issue because everything eventually comes down to how much one trusts God by embracing Jesus Christ. To do so is to accept His purpose as best, to be willing to wait for His timing, to embrace His ways, and to pursue His will.

When we perceive the written Word as the "truth," we are susceptible to the trap of fact, which is often used to avoid faith. We moderns are easily tempted to fall into the scientific mode, trying to prove what we believe by arguing the claims of the Bible, and doing so with emotional reactions to those who disagree. I like Christian apologetics. To read well-written logical and rational arguments for the biblical account of the birth, life, death, and resurrection of Jesus massages my logical instincts and stirs my sense of "truth". Lee Strobel's recent books, *The Case for Christi*[43] and *The Case for Faith,*[44] are good examples. I have recommended them to more than one person struggling with the intellectual and rational challenges raised by the enemies of faith.

The recent discoveries by scientists and archeologists that validate the biblical version of our origins and bring overwhelming evidence that there is a superior designer behind all life forms are inspiring to me. The interpretation of the DNA code has answered many questions and raised many more. But there is no longer any question of species ancestry that questions the accuracy of 1 Corinthians 15:39: "All flesh is not the same: Men have one kind of flesh, animals have another, birds another and fish another." The Hadron super collider has surprised empirical scientists with its irrefutable evidence of a creation moment with multiple dimensions at play.

We have suffered so long under the general attitude in society that to believe in a Creator is stupid because it does not measure

---

[43] Lee Strobel, *The Case For Christ* (Grand Rapids: Zondervan, 1998).
[44] Lee Strobel, *The Case for Faith* (Grand Rapids: Zondervan, 2000).

up to scientific evidence. Now, with the vast and growing amount of empirical evidence to support the claims of the Bible, along with a phenomenal number of archeological artifacts to support its narrative, it would seem that any logical person would become a believer. But it will not happen easily, because in spite of the integrity contained in the written word, the results of scientific research, and archeological discoveries, truth is found only in one's relationship with Christ.

To recognize truth in the living Christ is to live in relationship to Him and not just to interpret and apply the Bible to life. In fact, only when we seek to know God through Christ do we begin to appreciate the truth of the Word. It is essentially an issue of what (who) is at the center. At first, for those who have been raised on a diet of Bible-centered faith, to suggest a change of focus to a Christ-centered faith raises the specter of rejection of the Bible and opens the door to cheap grace. But in fact, what develops is an integrity with the Word in which grace becomes not only costly but real.

A classic illustration is the sexuality debate that is rocking the church these days. Not only is the gay-lesbian issue bringing fracturing stress on denominations, but also right behind are the issues of live-in relationships, young couples who choose to cohabitate rather than marry and senior adults who live together without marrying in order to avoid losing Social Security income, transgender issues, and so on. The authority-of-scripture solution is often held out as the final word. The problem is that while scripture has clear passages condemning some practices, it is not exhaustive on the issue. Many questionable practices and involvements today are not even mentioned in scripture. Perhaps that is because the issue of scripture, especially the New Testament, is not the rule of law but the reign of Christ from the cross. To hold out scriptural passages as the final authority is to suggest that making a rule with a code for enforcing it will bring about the truth of God. But if that could work, then Jesus didn't have to come. In the end, if there is to be any peace and healing in these emotional issues, we will discover that truth is found in the person of Christ.

Truth is not something to believe, it is someone to know. When a congregation believes that God is sovereign, that his ways are past finding out,[45] that in all things God works for the good of those who love him according to His purpose,[46] and that Jesus is the truth,[47] it has a radical impact on everything that fellowship will become. Sensing the Spirit and surrendering to God's will becomes more important than traditions, forms, codes, and interpretations.

As is sometimes said, the seven last words of the church are, "We never did it that way before," indicating how difficult it is for change in tradition or process to take place in the church. When the sovereignty of God is exercised in trust in the grace of Christ, a congregation experiences community instead of conflict and unity instead of division. More important, a congregation becomes a place of truth evidenced by the Spirit's presence as they extend to all "love, joy, peace, patience, kindness, goodness, faithfulness, gentleness and self-control" (Galatians 5:22–23).

---

[45] "How great is God—beyond our understanding! The number of his years is past finding out" (Job 36:26).

[46] "And we know that in all things God works for the good of those who love him, who have been called according to his purpose" (Romans 8:28, NIV).

[47] "Jesus told him, "I am the way, the truth, and the life" (John 14:6, NLT).

CHAPTER 14

Grace

It is by grace.
—Ephesians 2:5

A humorous account of a pastor sharing a moment with children in a worship service reflects the response some people have to the message of grace. He begins by asking a question: "What is gray, has a bushy tail, runs up and down trees, and stores nuts away for the winter?"

One small child, waving his hand, said, "I know, I know! The answer is Jesus, but it sounds like a squirrel to me."

We laugh at the honesty of a child who has been taught that certain words are the correct answer, even when it seems odd. So often, we do the same thing, especially with the language of faith. Words such as *love, truth,* and *grace* have major theological meaning but may be without substance in the mind of the believer. When confronted with questions of faith, we know the answer is love, truth, or grace, but it sounds like religion to us. For a theology of healing to be effective, it requires people of faith both understand and exercise grace. This means the theology of grace must have a practical application element, or it will fall into a theological crack.

The common definition of *grace* is "unmerited favor with God." That is accurate, but it is only one side of *grace.* The practical impact of Pentecost results in followers of Christ translating *grace* into relational lifestyles. By exercising *grace* in how we live together in the church, love becomes real and healing occurs. For that to happen in a fellowship, an important transformation in perceptions of holiness often have to transpire. The common assumption may be biblically sound, that when we experience righteousness as a gift of grace, we will respond naturally with a morally upright lifestyle. However, if that understanding of holiness is perceived to exist primarily within oneself, then there will be a focus on "personal morality" in isolation.

In isolated holiness, one feels righteous because of personal avoidance of moral sins (such as adultery, murder, stealing, etc.), and a sense of holiness is experienced through participation in spiritual activities such as worship and reading the Bible. This is a dangerous perception of holiness, for it is conceived and carried out in the isolation of one's own self. As we shall see, holiness should always be a community experience for people of God. For past generations, doctrinal righteousness ruled where believing the right doctrine was often perceived as essential for being righteous. But given the nature of user-friendly religion today, such doctrinal righteousness has given way to other concepts, such as the power of positive thinking, the media-driven church, or the emphasis on claiming God's promises for a trouble-free life.

While those (and other criteria as well) may be true and important, they are not the whole story. The problem is they are contained within one's own self and will fail the litmus test of Jesus's new commandment. Grace, righteousness, morality, and love are real only when they are exercised in relationship with others. Jesus underlined that reality with emphasis in his new commandment, for it is couched in the language of others: "Love one another." Therefore, critical to the healing of individuals as well as congregations is the transformation from a focus on self to the priority of others.

Virtually all the disaster in the contemporary Christian

community, whether it be the damaging of individuals or the wounding of a congregation, is the direct result of a failure on the part of church leaders and members to fulfill the "others" aspect of righteousness. Conversely, the degree to which healing can take place in individuals and in congregations is in direct proportion to the willingness of leaders and individuals to remove their sight from personal agendas, doctrines, causes, issues, and all the other forms of hamartia that can damage the church. The realigned focus on the wounds, needs, and care of others must become paramount. Jesus said, "all men will know you are my disciples if you love one another."[48]

The transition from self-focus to other focus is never easy. For people of all ages and in most societies, it requires major surgery, because it is a heart issue. The self is deeply entrenched into our every aspect of meaning and purpose. To set self aside in favor of others defies the most natural human response. Making this shift is a fundamental shift in human behavior. It requires an inside-out transformation that begins in the mind. When Paul wrote to the Romans to be "transformed by the renewing of your mind" (Romans 12:2), he was talking about the decision to change the focus of the "will," which is often referred to in scriptures as the "heart."

This transition is perhaps more difficult to achieve than ever before in the church in America today, primarily because we have increasingly become a society of individuals. Personal rights, entitlements, self-esteem, the right to choose, and other modern ideas dominate the mind-set of our culture, while concern for the common good seems to be disappearing. The individual is the king or queen.[49] Increasingly, ethics is defined as whatever benefits the individual.[50] The impact of this philosophy on the church has been dramatic. This fragmentation that marks our society is in

---

[48] John 13:35
[49] John Naisbett, *Megatrends* (New York: Morrow, 1990), 298–300.
[50] William Easum, *Dancing with Dinosaurs* (Arlington: Nashville, 1993), 28.

full bloom in the church today. As Leith Anderson notes, "Our increasingly pluralistic and fragmented churches are multiplying the list of unrealistic expectations people bring with them to worship. There are fewer individuals who have a sense of the whole and more who are bent on their special interest."[51] The result is that many of today's congregations are made up of individuals who are seeking some kind of healing for their disjointed lifestyles, fractured relationships, and fragile spirituality. It is a picture of the wounded church.

How can such a congregation develop a new vision that will empower it to have a lifestyle of grace? The answer is to learn that the most effective way to solve one's own needs and problems is to focus on serving others. Motivating a congregation to focus on others is perhaps the most difficult task leaders face today.[52] It requires modeling on the part of pastors and leaders, and a consistent teaching of some essential practical steps. Two practical exercises transform grace from a doctrine into a root of all healing relationships. The two are *understanding* and *forgiving*.

Habit number five of Steven Covey's book written for business executives is to "Seek first to understand, then to be understood."[53] It is an excellent summary of a critical spiritual exercise necessary to begin the healing process in the church. Learning to practice this simple formula results in fulfillment of the new commandment of Jesus to "love one another." Unfortunately, often the problem is that our natural way of thinking is by the reverse process of "seeking first to be understood." Thus, the first step of catching a new vision is to remove self from the center of our focus and, by an

---

[51] Leith Anderson, *A Church for the 21st Century* (Minneapolis: Bethany, 1992), 72.

[52] George Barna, *User Friendly Churches* (Ventura: Regal Books, 1991), 26–27.

[53] Steven Covey, *The 7 Habits of Highly Effective People* (New York: Simon & Schuster), 235–260.

act of the will (heart), decide to do what is necessary to understand the needs of the other person.

It is not an easy task. The need to win, and the drive to succeed at the expense of others, is so powerfully entrenched in our self-identification that it often takes a miracle of grace to love others. Our debates, arguments, and positioning over issues are all about insisting that the other person understand us first. Jesus's mandate has a blessed twist in that when we operate by self first, we become the walking wounded. But when we love others in priority over selves, we experience healing of the very center of ourselves.

The lie of the serpent in the Garden of Eden was counter to this: "Eat the forbidden fruit and you will be like God." In other words, you will be free of rules because you will be self-directed. It was a lie because, instead of experiencing freedom, Adam and Eve fell into the bondage of focusing on self (hamartia) instead of on God's will. The more we think about self first, the greater our bondage and the deeper the wounding. Jesus reverses the lie with the truth. You will experience healing of yourself in direct proportion to the degree you *understand* the other person and then respond with healing love.

The major cause of conflict in churches often begins with failing to "seek first to understand." Moving from an environment of judgment of others, criticism, gossip, exclusion, and all the other characteristics that mark a wounded and wounding fellowship to one of healing and renewal requires an intentional effort to understand the other person.

The first level of understanding has to do with general perceptions, such as detecting the needs of others. Leaders of the church-growth movement have correctly identified *need identification* as a prerequisite to program design. Baby boomers have been the primary focus of need identification, for they are the major missing link in the church as a unique generation. Much of the change in worship styles and program emphasis today is an attempt to provide a church that fits the needs of that generation.[54] Contemporary songs (instead of hymns), drama, and family-oriented programs are examples. Even the kind and duration of sermons is determined by need analysis, although there are significant differences of opinion in what that really means. One expert says that in our nonsequential world, every sermon will have to stand alone, making sermons in series obsolete.[55] Another says that baby boomers will judge a sermon's value by its biblical content. Therefore, expository preaching will connect better than topical sermons.[56] Understanding the needs of those both inside and outside the church and responding to those needs is an important first step in bringing healing and wholeness to a congregation.

The higher step in this element of grace is to listen intently to the story of the other person. Everyone on earth has a story. The question is, will they feel safe enough to tell their story, and if they do, will it be heard? To understand the other person requires the receiver to be a true listener. Communication experts agree that true listening is rare but is a critical key to understanding. The Bible agrees: "My dear brothers, take note of this: Everyone should be quick to listen, slow to speak" (James 1:19). Our natural responses are to listen in order to reply, often with a correction or evaluation of what has just been said. While the other person is speaking, we often are preparing to speak by filtering everything that is said through our own paradigms and experiences. Our replies, then, are really an attempt to be understood ourselves, and as a result, we never really understand what's going on with the other person.

To really listen in order to understand requires *empathic* listening.[57] Empathic listening requires you to discover the other

---

[54] Anderson, 63–65.
[55] Ibid, 45.
[56] Herb Miller, *Connecting with God* (Nashville: Abingdon, 1994), 90.
[57] Covey, 239–243.

person's frame of reference, to see the world through his or her eyes, to feel the emotions that drive the other person, and to understand how he or she feels and why the person feels the way he or she does. It requires setting aside all judgments, rejections, and conditions so that empathy, not sympathy, occurs for the other person. The incarnation of Jesus Christ becomes the ultimate example of this critical activity. He actively loved us to the point that he set aside His divine stature and status to become human. As a result, He understands the feelings and emotions with which we live, and what it is like to face life every day with the certainty of death at the end. "He took up our infirmities and carried our diseases"(Matthew 8:17). "For this reason he had to be made like his brothers in every way, in order that he might become a merciful and faithful high priest in service to God, and that he might make atonement for the sins of the people" (Hebrews 2:17). "For we do not have a high priest who is unable to sympathize with our weaknesses, but we have one who has been tempted in every way, just as we are—yet was without sin" (Hebrews 4:15). To develop the art of understanding is to exercise grace as a spiritual act of worship. It is how the believing community models Christ's incarnation. Without understanding, there is no grace, no healing.

When we seek to understand others first, our responses will be different. We begin to perceive the wounds and scars that script behavior, the personalities and emotional makeups that determine their actions and reactions, and the needs and perceptions that drive their searches for meaning. To walk in another's shoes becomes an experience of walking on holy ground. As the gospel hymn writer put it, "No one understands like Jesus, he's a friend beyond compare."[58] To be allowed to understand another is to be allowed to touch that person's soul. It is to see people through the eyes of the Savior. Such understanding opens the door of love, for the response of those led by the Spirit of God will always be one

---

[58] "No One Understands Like Jesus" by John Peterson, copyright 1952.

of compassion and mercy. It will enable the listener to see beyond the harsh words, the aberrant behavior, the coarse language, the immoral lifestyle, to see the soul created in the image of God. Instead of reacting with rejection (the major causes of wounding and division in the church), there will be a great desire to bring wholeness. The qualities of love will become dominant: patience, kindness, acceptance, protection, trust, hope, perseverance, faithfulness. When that happens healing is possible as the door is opened to the next step of grace, which is forgiveness.

Chapter 15

Forgiveness

Forgive us our debts, as we also have forgiven our debtors.
—Matthew 6:12

Few Old Testament stories expose the nature and rewards of forgiveness as does that of Joseph. The pride of his father Jacob's eye, and the object of hatred by his brothers, he is sold into bondage to a caravan of traders and ends up as a servant in Egypt. Injustice follows him at every turn. Because of his sense of loyalty and a personal character of righteousness, he rejects the advances of his employer's wife, is unjustly accused, and ends up in the dungeon where he languishes for years, a forgotten victim. In that dark place of cruelty, hardship, and abuse, he comes to believe in the justice of God. It is an amazing response of an abused young man that contradicts the natural inclination of victim mentality. Being the victim of abuse does not guarantee that one has to live in a prison of emotional and social malfunction.

When at last Joseph is delivered from prison, it is with an amazing elevation to the highest position in the land, second only to the king. But the story does not end there. The famine that engulfs the region impacts his family back home in Canaan. His father sends his brothers to Egypt in search of food for the family. Completely unaware that the royal authority in charge of disposition of the food reserves is none other than their spurned brother, the brothers become victim to his toying with their emotions. At first it appears to be a story of justice being played out in the normal human sense of some bad boys getting what they deserved. But in the end, Joseph treats them with gracious and loving care, announcing that their treatment of him was according to God's will and, in the end, a great blessing for all.

The biblical account of Joseph affords many lessons. For Bible historians it reveals how the children of Israel ended up in Egypt where they became the victims of a cruel pharaoh. For moralists, Joseph's response reveals the kind of character that rises above the norm. His decisions are rooted in a value system that transcends normal human behavior. For psychologists, it is a powerful model for how a victim can overcome the devastation of abuse and injustice to become a healthy adult. But for followers of Christ, it is a pre-Christ revelation of the power of forgiveness to redeem, heal and transform. Forgiveness is one of the great gifts from God that is often misunderstood and therefore rejected.

At the heart of grace is God's forgiveness of our sins through the sacrifice of Christ. To be forgiven is the ultimate experience of grace. To forgive others is the ultimate act of love. It is worth noting that when Jesus uttered the prayer we know as the Lord's prayer, the only part He had commentary on was the phrase "forgive us our debts as we forgive our debtors" (Matthew 6:12). He added, "If you forgive men when they sin against you, your heavenly Father will also forgive you. But if you do not forgive men their sins, your Father will not forgive your sin" (Matthew 6:14–15). It is a radical yet fundamentally important statement that emphasizes the critical importance of the experience of being forgiven and of forgiving. In regard to our own need for salvation, to be forgiven is the trigger for the move into a relationship with God, receiving his Spirit. To be forgiven by God is to be set free from the guilt and consequences of sin. It is an action that God conducts on our behalf. We are utterly incapable of providing our own salvation. Only God is able to do that for us.

However, there is more to forgiveness than what God does for us in removing from us the stain of guilt. What does it mean to be forgiven? Some may mistake forgiveness to mean that God views our sins as having never happened and simply removes that part of our personal history. Such thinking denies the reality of both our sin and of God's action of forgiveness. It is forgiveness that removes the guilt and the condemnation and opens the way for a critical change at the heart of who we are so that we are transformed. It is a primary principle of the way God works, and it is effective for individuals and for congregations that need to experience forgiveness for their past history and for a renewal for their future.

The catch is that forgiveness received without forgiveness given is void. The condition Jesus put on forgiveness means that the believer's forgiving others is a critical element in becoming like Him. We note that in Matthew 6:13–15, the word translated "sin" is not hamartia, "missing the mark," but *paraptomata*, "a violence or a violation of your person." It speaks of the kind of action taken by another that causes us to experience hurt, to feel damaged, and usually results in the reaction of defending yourself. *Paraptomata* is the kind of violation that often elicits feelings of revenge in the natural man. It is more difficult for us to forgive *paraptomata* than hamartia. When someone "misses the mark" (hamartia*)*, we say, "Oh, we have to excuse her. She is just misguided."

But when we are violated (*paraptomata*), that is another story. The call to "forgive as we are forgiven" becomes far more difficult and seriously challenges our ability to love. Perhaps that is connected to our penchant to adopt a legalistic model of spirituality in our struggle with concepts of grace. "Eye for eye" (Exodus 21:24) makes more sense to the natural mind. We find in the idea of justice a feeling of security, that God is invested in fairness and equity. All of this is the fallacy of the self-centered mind. Our mistaken idea of justice is often what we expect God to do to those who do not treat us as we want. It is backward, the opposite from God's definition of justice. According to the ancient prophets, justice is what we do in our treatment of others. "He has showed you, O man, what is good. And what does the LORD require of you? To act justly and to love mercy and to walk humbly with your God." To "act justly" is not to call down the judgment of God on others for how they treat us but the divine expectation that we will treat others with grace, compassion, fairness, truth, honor, and love.

To demand justice from God as a way of exercising judgment on others is to give evidence that we don't understand the idea of grace or forgiveness, for if God exercises justice instead of grace and mercy, none of us has a chance. However, justice is one of the flawless qualities of God. Not only did He demand that the Israelites be just in their relationships with one another, including the stranger and the foreigner, He exercised His justice on them for failure to be a people of justice. The scriptures are replete with references to His perfect justice. One of the complaints of Job was "I am innocent, but God denies me justice" (Job 34:5), to which the Sovereign Lord replies, "Would you discredit my justice? Would you condemn me to justify yourself?" (Job 40:8). There are numerous references in the Psalms to the justice of God as one of his characteristics: "The LORD is known by his justice" (Psalm 9:16). "Your throne, O God, will last for ever and ever; a scepter of justice will be the scepter of your kingdom" (Psalm 45:6). "Righteousness and justice are the foundation of your throne; love and faithfulness go before you" (Psalm 89:14). The prophets echo that identity of God: "But the LORD Almighty will be exalted by his justice, and the holy God will show himself holy by his righteousness" (Isaiah 5:16); "A bruised reed he will not break, and a smoldering wick he will not snuff out. In faithfulness he will bring forth justice" (Isaiah 42:3). Matthew quotes Isaiah in identifying the mission of Jesus as one of justice: "Here is my servant whom I have chosen, the one I love, in whom I delight; I will put my Spirit on him, and he will proclaim justice to the nations ... A bruised reed he will not break, and a smoldering wick he will not snuff out, till he leads justice to victory" (Matthew 12:18, 20).

It is the justice of God that results in our forgiveness. The epistle to the Romans is a carefully scripted explanation of the justice and forgiveness of God at work on behalf of his creation. After emphasizing the fact that we are utterly incapable of fulfilling the law, and are therefore objects of God's wrath, it explains how God exercises His justice in a way that allows us to be counted as righteous, that is to be forgiven, even though we are guilty. "But now a righteousness from God, apart from law, has been made known, to which the Law and the Prophets testify. This righteousness from God comes through faith in Jesus Christ to all who believe. There is no difference, for all have sinned and fall short of the glory of God, and are justified freely by his grace through the redemption that came by Christ Jesus. God presented him as a sacrifice of atonement, through faith in his blood. He did this to demonstrate his justice, because in his forbearance he had left the sins committed beforehand unpunished—he did it to demonstrate his justice at the present time, so as to be just and the one who justifies those who have faith in Jesus" (Romans 3:21–26).

Contrary to our common understanding of justice, in God's system of righteousness to act justly is to act on behalf of others in order to set them free from the consequences of their *paraptomata* (violence) against us. This often results in the victim paying the price, a sacrifice, on behalf of the guilty person. While it seems unfair, and is contrary to our sense of "righteousness," it is the way of divine justice, and it is the basis of true forgiveness. To forgive as we have been forgiven is to cancel the debt of the other person, even to pay the price that they can never repay. Forgiveness is never merited, or it would not be forgiveness. Forgiveness is never repayable, or it is never forgiveness. The only way we can repay the forgiveness of God, who exercised His judgment on the innocent Lamb so that we could walk away from the offering being counted as righteous, is to act that same way toward the people in our lives who need our forgiveness. We can never forgive God back, for He is holy and does not need forgiveness.

But there is more to forgiveness than accepting God's gracious gift. By it, we are not only counted as righteous but also are set on the path of healing. To both experience and exercise forgiveness is essential to the healing process of our personal lives, of our homes and marriages, and of our congregations. Jesus knew that personal healing, as well as the healing of a wounded fellowship, takes both kinds of forgiveness. When we ask God for forgiveness, we receive it gladly, and the healing process of our heart and soul is set into motion. It is always good to be forgiven! It is sometimes another story when we are called to forgive. However, it is equally good to forgive. In giving us the mandate to forgive, Jesus introduced us to the secret of living free from the bondage of emotional prisons. To forgive another is to liberate yourself.

When we are victims of injustice or cruelty and are wounded, we are in bondage to the emotions of anti-love until we forgive. The emotions generated by not forgiving are the same as the love-destroying characteristics of 1 Corinthians 13: envy, boasting, pride, rudeness, self-pity, anger, resentment, and revenge. Ephesians 4:31 describes them as bitterness, rage, anger, brawling, slander, and malice. They are not only the major weapons of war in divided congregations used to wound one another, but also they are the balls and chains of the soul. As long as any reactionary, negative, anti-love emotion is in place, the soul is in bondage. The member who is angry at another and begins to hold bitterness in their heart and mind has become a slave to that emotion and is being manipulated by the words and deeds of the other person. So long as we are in that kind of bondage, we are being wounded and are wounding others. We can never become whole or experience healing until we are liberated from that source of bondage.

Deliverance is experienced at the cross of forgiveness. When the offended one is forgiven, then freedom is experienced. That is why Jesus placed such a strong emphasis on forgiving others. By letting go of the demands for justice, giving up expectations for restitution or compensation, the victim experiences healing. In exercising forgiveness, they pry open the doors of their hearts to grace, not only for their own healing processes and deliverances from the bondage of sin but also for their becoming vessels of grace and healing to others, including the perceived perpetrator. To forgive an injustice or a violation, and to do so with the kind of love Jesus demonstrated, is to take a step closer to Calvary. Of course it is not easy. That is because it is a way of "taking up our crosses." It means that what was cherished has died, but in the end, what is of more important has come to life. It can be observed that in those congregations that have experienced recovery and renewal after a painful division, healing has been triggered by active forgiveness of others.

The congregational lifestyle of forgiveness is a critical element in the church being true to its calling in the twenty-first century. This is a big order, but given the chaotic trend of ecclesiastical division, it is necessary. If Robert Wuthnow's prediction that the "great schism in the church today over social issues will be much greater than the divisions of the past over doctrinal issues, creating a canyon of separation so deep that a new order for the church is in the near future"[59] is true, then there will be increasing numbers of congregations that may misfire and suffer internal failure. When that happens not only will the people of those fellowships suffer deep wounding, but the body of Christ will be impotent in fulfilling the role of being vessels of grace to a fractured world. The ministry of healing hinges on the power of forgiveness.

Forgiveness is the critical element of grace. It must penetrate and flow through every aspect of the church life, whether it is different personalities on a committee or the attitude of saints toward struggling seekers. It is the daily function of the ekklesia. It is the primary ingredient in the unity of the fellowship. It is the way of the cross of Christ.

---

[59] Wuthnow would be proven wrong if grace and forgiveness become the nature of the church.

CHAPTER 16

Mercy

For I desire mercy, not sacrifice, and acknowledgment of God
rather than burnt offerings.
—Hosea 6:6

A fundamental point in the theology of healing is the conviction
that God's redemptive work in Christ Jesus was intended to
benefit the whole world. That is precisely the parameter of John
3:16, "For God so loved the world that he gave his one and only
Son, that whoever believes in him shall not perish but have eternal
life." The question is, who is included in "world" and "whoever"?
Is God committed to the salvation of the world, or does he intend
to rescue only a small number of selected people from hell and
judgment? Is the mercy of God deep and wide, or does it hang by
a slender thread of history?[60]

It seems that a fear of many evangelicals is that if we are too
diverse or inclusive, we will lose our holy character and ultimately
our standing with God. From where does that kind of fear and
criteria come? Perhaps it is a worry over becoming pluralistic,
embracing every belief so that we lose the heart and soul of our
Christian theology. More likely it is fostered by a false idea of
evangelical Christianity, one that seeks to protect Christ, or

---

[60] Clark Pinnock, *A Wideness in God's Mercy* (Grand Rapids: Zondervan), 18.

preserve the sanctity of the church, or even protect one's own salvation by creating a holy environment. It does not come from an understanding of the heart of the God of love, nor from a biblical exegesis of his mercy. When a narrowing of the mercy of God dominates our theology and resultant view of the church, not only is Christ maligned, but also judgmentalism replaces love and exclusivism supplants evangelical passion. It is the very exclusivism warned against in the gospel.

Clark Pinnock observes that "what seems to have happened is that Christians have picked up the very exclusivism warned against in the gospel. Jesus himself rejected the notion that election confers privileged status and is the basis of superiority. God's kingdom is not the place for those who want to protect their own salvation in opposition to the salvation of others. There is no basis in the gospel for viewing outsiders suspiciously, holding them at arms length, or for being fearful lest the unclean be saved. Pharisees are not exclusively Jewish legalists, for the identical tendency is dominant in Christianity and other religions as well."[61]

We do not deny the claims of Christ and abdicate to pluralism when we show mercy. On the contrary, given the fractured and isolated nature of our society, it is reasonable to assume that the need of the multitude is to experience acceptance, tolerance, and inclusion. Symbolic of the brokenness that afflicts our culture is the isolation that accompanies the drive for autonomy. If humanity is created for relationship, then a culture that encourages individualism to the point of isolation effects a violence on the people of that culture. That kind of focus on individual rights is quite the opposite of the emphasis of the new command to love one another.[62] In the environment of love, not only is there a

---

[61] Ibid, p. 41.

[62] Lesslie Newbigin, *Foolishness to the Greeks* (Grand Rapids: Eerdmans, 1986), .21–41. Newbigin argues that the idea of a government that established and protected individual rights was incomprehensible to the Hebrew, Latin, Greek, or Arabic cultures.

commitment to understanding and a liberation in forgiving, but also there must be a willingness to accept some things that are not clearly understood and that at first may be difficult to accept. That is the nature of mercy.

The scriptures burn with the message of mercy. On the one hand we are reminded that it is not by the righteous deeds we have done, but because of the mercy of God that we are saved. On the other hand, the judgment of God falls heavily on those who do not show mercy to others. "For I desire mercy, not sacrifice, and acknowledgment of God rather than burnt offerings" (Hosea 6:6). "He has showed you, O man, what is good. And what does the LORD require of you? To act justly and to love mercy and to walk humbly with your God" (Micah 6:8).

Jesus echoes the conditional nature of mercy. In his Sermon on the Mount, he puts it in a positive mandate: "Blessed are the merciful, for they will be shown mercy" (Matt. 5:7). He challenged the cold hearts of the Pharisees with his parables. The question about who is my neighbor, implying a limit to the scope of mercy, was answered with the parable of the good Samaritan. Jesus then asked which traveler was the wounded man's neighbor. Luke 10:37 records the answer: "The expert in the law replied, 'The one who had mercy on him.' Jesus told him, 'Go and do likewise.'" It seems that to refuse to extend mercy to another person is something like chopping a hole in the bottom of your lifeboat in order to not have to rescue another passenger.

Mercy is different from forgiveness in that when we forgive another person, it has a powerful personal benefit in our deliverance from emotional bondage. But when we extend mercy to another, it is the other person who is impacted. The one who is merciful does so not for his or her own benefit but in order to help the other person. It becomes a challenge when the other person is guilty of an offense. Mercy usually involves a sacrifice, a suffering on behalf of the other person. It is mercy because it is done voluntarily. It is mercy because it is not a retaliation, or an act of justice. It is mercy because it is a response of compassion.

Mercy can be costly, is often painful, and requires complete trust in God. Only by trusting in God's ultimate justice, an extension of His sovereignty, is it possible to give up all claims for justice and extend mercy in its place. Mercy becomes the pure form of love, the supreme act of submission. To extend mercy to the impure, the defiled, the corrupted, the diseased, the crippled, the blind, and the oppressed is to live and act with the same vision and purpose that marked the life and ministry of Jesus Christ. It is impossible to liberate, release, and heal without mercy. Mercy applied is the willingness to see the sin of others as evidence of their great need, to accept the injustices of life as opportunities to exercise grace, and to look past the offensiveness of another and see the soul of an individual originally created in God's image.

Israel's refusal to be a people of mercy was at the root of God's contention with them. Their idolatry of sacrificing to the pagan gods of the land was evidence of their failure to know and worship Jehovah God. That was a repeated offense to the Lord God Almighty. But it was their abandonment of mercy that gave evidence of their hardened hearts—and that was odious to God. The measuring stick of their worship and the evidence of their heart against His ways was not, in God's eyes, in their sacrifice or ritual but in their failure to act with mercy. That message is repeated in the prophets: "For I desire mercy, not sacrifice, and acknowledgment of God rather than burnt offerings" (Hosea 6:6). "He has showed you, O man, what is good. And what does the LORD require of you? To act justly and to love mercy and to walk humbly with your God" (Micah 6:8). "This is what the LORD Almighty says: 'Administer true justice; show mercy and compassion to one another'" (Zech. 7:9).

Jesus brings to the new covenant the same root issue, calling the people of God to be a people of mercy. In his Sermon on the Mount he said it very simply and straightforward: "Blessed are the merciful, for they will be shown mercy" (Matt. 5:7). Like so many of the promises of happiness and blessing, it is rooted in a condition: it is in extending mercy to others that we experience God's mercy. When the Pharisees criticized Him for eating with unclean people Jesus tells them to explain what Hosea 6:6 means where Jehovah announces, "I desire mercy, not sacrifice." Before they can retort, Jesus answers them with a self-proclamation about his mission: "For I have not come to call the righteous, but sinners" (Matt. 9:13). If the church is the living body of Christ on earth, designed and empowered through the ages to continue his ministry of healing wounded people with the ministry of redemption, renewal, and restoration, then it is essential that mercy be an intentional root of the fellowship. That seemed to be a concern of James, who wrote that "judgment without mercy will be shown to anyone who has not been merciful. Mercy triumphs over judgment!" and that "the wisdom that comes from heaven is first of all pure; then peace-loving, considerate, submissive, full of mercy and good fruit, impartial and sincere" (James 2:13, 3:17).

The healthy church, and the individual who is secure in Christ, will enlarge their borders of mercy. The more the experience of being healed and restored to wholeness—the wider the scope of mercy will become. It is an interesting self-test of any congregation to recognize who is not made to feel welcome, who is made to feel like an outsider, who is excluded and rejected. The inquiry as to why will usually result in a time of repentance and petition for forgiveness. For it is the church, God's unique vessel of grace, that is His earthly model of mercy. As our culture heats up with more and more violence against people who are not understood or loved, and the numbers of people who believe they are beyond redemption increases, it becomes ever more critical that the church, the living body of Jesus Christ, exercise a wideness in God's mercy. If, as prophecy announces and current events indicate, publicly confessing faith in Christ will result in persecution and unjust abuse, then it is essential that the believer grasp and hold onto this fundamental nature of God. In a world of war and conflict, where ethnic cleansing and abuse dominates the news, it seems that the people who study the gospel, who claim to be forgiven by Christ, and who love to sing "Amazing Grace" would also have workshops and seminars on how to exercise mercy. It is the exercise of mercy that sets the followers of Christ apart from the world, apart from the religious zealots.

Part III
The Healing Impact

CHAPTER 17

Sensing the Spirit

And in him you too are being built together to become a dwelling
in which God lives by his Spirit.
—Ephesians 2:22

At the beginning of this book the question was asked, "What
constitutes a successful church?" Several elements of the answer to that
question have emerged as we have discussed the Christological mission
for which the church was ordained and the biblical roots upon which
the ekklesia stands. A working definition of a successful congregation
is one that reflects the nature of Christ, primarily in how they love one
another. A second answer is that a successful congregation is one that
exercises grace in how its members respond to heal the wounds and
needs of one another and its community. A third answer is the power
of transformation exhibited in individual lives, in the congregational
fellowship and in the surrounding community as grace is incarnated
from a doctrine of faith into a life-changing experience.

The commission Jesus gave to the church has not been
recalled. We are still in the business of proclaiming the gospel
of Christ. A successful congregation is one whose work is never
completed, an evangel forever impacted by the needs of men and
women trapped in the darkness of sin; and a discipler, constantly
in the business of bringing believers into a transformed maturity
in Christ. That is the work of healing. To lead individuals to

Christ is to introduce them to the great physician "who forgives all your sins and heals all your diseases" (Psalm 103:3). How that healing takes place will depend to a great degree upon the wellness of the fellowship, for it is through the loving care of a fellowship that personal transformation will come to completion.

The importance of a healthy fellowship as a change agent for individuals cannot be overstated. A church that is spiritually alive and healthy is aware of those who are wounded and in need of the savior, and is willing to change and flex, to sacrifice and surrender, in order to connect.[63] Transformed lives are the result of a sensitive, healing fellowship.

The ekklesia is a family of families. Today the marginalizing and disintegration of the home and the fracturing of marriages could be the most critical issue facing the church. The dysfunctional family is the cause of many of the wounds suffered by individuals both in and out of the church. Those families that are whole are families who exercise love, understanding, submission, and forgiveness that is needed to heal the broken soul. When families are not capable of that kind of relationship, it negatively impacts individuals, the church, and the community. Healthy congregations are family oriented because the concept of family is a primary element in God's design and purpose.[64]

---

[63] Easum. The thesis of his book is that for churches to avoid becoming dinosaurs (relics of the past), there has to be a willingness to change along with the culture. In pp. 25–33 he lists sixteen shifts happening in history which the successful church must consider.

[64] "Family" was the primary unit through which God blessed humans. It began with creation, was the basis for life in the nation Israel and the structure through which the Law was implemented. One only has to read the emphasis on generations and the begats to grasp how important the family connect is in God's eyes. That emphasis is carried into the new covenant where "family" is the primary component of the church (ekklesia). That concept of family is as important in the church as it was in Israel. "For this reason I kneel before the Father, from whom his whole family in heaven and on earth derives its name" (Ephesians 3:14, 15). "For it is time for judgment to begin with the family of God; and if it begins with us, what will the outcome be for those who do not obey the gospel of God?" (1 Peter 4:17).

The idea that an effective church is designed to relate to only one generation is heresy. If there are no older generations in a congregation, who will help the young believers grow in grace and avoid the mistakes of the past? Who will teach younger women how to be godly, the younger men how to avoid the pitfalls of masculine sin (hamartia) (1 Timothy 5, Titus 2)? Who will help the older generations to stay alive and avoid the dirge of doing everything "the same old way"?

The spirit of joy and celebration of younger generation music in the church has brought a fresh wind of praise. With the theology and worship of the older generation's music, a reverence and awe of God is maintained. Together, they create a wonderfully rich, new worship that the Spirit of God is using to stir the winds of renewal in the church. The ability of a local congregation to be an effective redeeming and healing agent to the people in the community requires inclusion that honors and appreciates all generations. For today's congregation, maintaining care of "family" requires a constant evaluation of the needs of each generation in the church and community with a willingness to adjust what and how ministry is done in order to respond to those needs. Precisely the same priorities that reveal God's design and purpose for the church, and that brings transforming renewal to local congregations, is that which brings healing to the family. Love, mutual submission, grace empowered by understanding and forgiveness, and a holy mercy that is willing to suffer the consequences on behalf of others are the spiritual substances of a healthy and growing family. It is the divine formula for healing all kinds of relationships, especially in the fellowship of believers. Further, it empowers that fellowship to be God's refuge and help for people in search of healing and hope.

The disaster of the conflicted congregation is not just the pain it suffers within its own ranks, but its inability to be the place of healing for individuals seeking refuge from the violence of sin. When a seeker enters a church that is wracked with division, instead of experiencing the healing power of grace, he or she experiences the damaging power of pride. Pride is at play when everything is always about "me." Self, the destructive core of pride, results in our always asking the question, "What do *I* want? What will you do for *me?*" instead of "What is God's will? What can I do for you?" Pride, the primary attitude that rejects the sovereignty of God, is always hanging around, looking for an opportunity to step in and divide.

It often appears that when the divine design and purpose for the church mandate is hidden under layers of organizational positions and religious systems, pride emerges triumphant. For example, the status given to "ordained" clergy can easily translate into a title of authority and superiority over the "laity." When that authority is seen as vested in a position of power rather than one of servant grace, then pride has usurped center stage, inevitably resulting in conflict and division.

How many times has a pastor fallen into the trap of letting the membership divide over his or her agenda? When any individual, be it the pastor, choir director, organist, song leader, Sunday school teacher, custodian, elder, deacon, or member, becomes the issue of the church, then hamartia (sin) is in full force. Christ has been displaced from the center and a war of wills rages into some form of conflict that ultimately will destroy the unity of that fellowship. The essential prevention of pride dominating the fellowship is to seek and sense the presence and leading of the Holy Spirit. When the Spirit of Christ is invited to work in the heart and will of the people, then a spirit of peace creates a fertile environment for the ministry of healing.

The instructions for worship and atonement given by God through Moses to be exercised in the tabernacle were carefully detailed. While the instructions provided for their immediate need of relationship with God and with one another, they were also a type of the person and work of Christ. Included in the details were instructions regarding the altar of "fragrant incense" that burned in the holy place, providing a sweet odor to anyone who would enter. On the Day of Atonement, as the high priest prepared to enter into the Holy of Holies to offer a sacrifice on behalf of the people, he would carry some of that burning "fragrant incense" into the place of atonement with him. Thus, the offering of atonement is referred to as a "fragrant" sacrifice to God.

That Old Testament "incense" is understood as a type, representative of the ministry of the Holy Spirit in the church. The works of inviting, intercession, guiding, encouraging, teaching, interpreting, and so on are ways the Holy Spirit today helps the community of faith present a true offering of grace to God. Paul called forth the image of the "fragrant incense" as he admonished believers to "live a life of love, just as Christ loved us and gave himself up for us as a fragrant offering and sacrifice to God" (Ephesians 5:2). Some liturgical churches use incense in their worship as a pungent reminder of the "Spirit" presence of God. Most evangelical churches long ago cast aside such practices, reasoning that it is not the burning of incense that pleases God but the presence of *koinonia*. *Koinonia* is the word used in the Greek text and is usually translated as "fellowship" in our English Bibles.[65] It is common for a church to use the word *fellowship* to describe any gathering related to the church, especially if there is food involved. That, however, is a corruption of the original meaning of *koinonia*.

Fellowship (*koinonia*) first appears in the New Testament in the immediate aftermath of the day of Pentecost. Acts 2:42 records four distinct devotions in the first congregation of believers: "They devoted themselves (1) to the apostles' teaching and (2) to the fellowship, (3) to the breaking of bread, and (4) to prayer." The apostles' teaching we understand as a sharing, learning process. The breaking of bread was a reference to sharing

---

[65] TDNT, Vol. III, 797–809.

the Lord's table together (not church potlucks!). Prayer was the ongoing conversation with God that they seemed to do naturally. But what constitutes fellowship?

Fellowship (*koinonia*) is what happens to a congregation when there is an intentional invitation to the Holy Spirit to be the active, motivating, guiding power in the life of that congregation. While I do not discredit the validity of signs and wonders and the many "miracles, tongues, and healings" as evidence of the presence of the Holy Spirit, they do not represent His ultimate power. When the resurrected Jesus promised the anointing of the Spirit with power, it was so His followers would have the ability to witness to the reality of His person and mission.[66] The ultimate "sign and wonder" of the Holy Spirit is His power of transformation. It is expressed in the word *koinonia*. The transformation of a diverse, needy, wounded, sinful people, once dominated by the wounded self with their driving needs of pride, power, and possessions, into a loving, healing, devoted fellowship where Christ is Lord is the "burning incense" that is a sweet-smelling offering to God. It is utterly impossible for that to happen without the powerful presence of the Spirit.

Koinonia, for a holy, healthy, and healing fellowship, is the "fragrant incense" of the presence of the Spirit of Christ. It is an aroma of peace that becomes evident to all who enter and experience the Spirit in the midst of the congregation. Words such as "peaceful," "warm," "accepting," "loving," and "real" often are spoken by those who detect its aroma for the first time. It is not something that can be programmed. Signing up couples to track down visitors to shake their hands is a good practice, but it does not guarantee *koinonia*. Wearing name tags and having coffee following worship will also help, but it won't make

---

[66] Acts 1:8: "But you will receive power when the Holy Spirit comes on you; and you will be my witnesses in Jerusalem, and in all Judea and Samaria, and to the ends of the earth." The word for power, *dunamis*, is translated in other places as "ability."

koinonia happen. Singing only upbeat music or preaching longer, or shorter, sermons isn't the key. Those are all worthy activities to do, but they are effective only when we are aware that *koinonia* transpires by the Holy Spirit. When He is allowed to move like a breeze through the gathering, He brings to reality the kind of love that imitates Christ.

Koinonia begins to happen when believers are willing to allow the Spirit to trigger works of love. When the lifestyle of forgiveness, of sacrificial submission, of genuinely seeking to understand, of unconditional acceptance of others, and of the exercise of mercy is pursued, then *koinonia* invades all the areas of the church like the odor of burning incense. It is the Spirit who convicts and calls to repentance. It is the Spirit who encourages and provides abilities and dedication to serve. It is the Spirit who removes the prison bars from our own hearts when we forgive. It is the Spirit who empowers us to set aside our grievances and demands for justice and, instead, exercise mercy. It is the Spirit who heals, for the Spirit is the Spirit of Christ who is the Great Physician. The Spirit is the one who brings about the peace of Christ and who gives gifts to men and women for ministry, thereby baptizing the fellowship with the power of grace.

A successful church is one that is given power by the Spirit of peace. It is a success that is marked by four distinct works of Christ incarnated into the life of the congregation. The first is the mandate to love in that Christ-like manner that empowered Him to accept and value everyone without hate or condemnation. Second is the power of truth, which acts on an unwavering trust and confidence in the sovereign will of God prevailing in history. Third is the covenant of grace that is passed on to the community of believers as the power to understand and forgive. The fourth work of Christ that marks the fellowship of peace is the cross of mercy. Like Jesus, people of *koinonia* are willing to give up and give away what is dearest to them, purely for the sake and benefit of others. It is a painful exercise that results in a powerful peace.

Mother Teresa captures the path whereby peace becomes the lifestyle of a congregation.

The Simple Path
The fruit of silence is *prayer.*
The fruit of prayer is *faith.*
The fruit of faith is *love.*
The fruit of love is *service.*
The fruit of service is *peace.*[67]

---

[67] Lucinda Vardey, *Mother Teresa: A Simple Path* (New York: Ballantine Books, 1995), 1.

CHAPTER 18

First Things First

Seek first his kingdom and his righteousness.
—Matthew 6:33

In Sri Lanka there is a Buddhist temple, appropriately called the Temple of the Tooth. Once a year a major ceremony occurs, accompanied with great devotion and respect. A small casket is opened up, and a smaller casket is removed. It then is opened, revealing a yet smaller container, which is opened, revealing another smaller one. This continues until a seventh casket is removed. It is then opened up to reveal a single tooth. It is identified as a tooth from the great Buddha, and the faithful observe it with reverence and awe. The reason for the reverence of the tooth is that the words of Buddha flowed over it. The ritual is concluded with a ceremonious reencasement of the tooth inside the seven caskets, where it will again be hidden away for another year.[68]

Have important elements of "being the church" been buried under layers of ecclesiastical wrappings? Have we come to value trinkets and symbols of the church more than the ekklesia (body of Christ) itself? A visit to the local Christian bookstore suggests so, as religious trinkets and Christian fiction now occupy more

---

[68] This story was told at a retreat in Seattle by the Chaplain of Westmont College in which he related his visit to the Temple of the Tooth.

space than theological works. Do more people read books about the Book than read the Book itself? Are we guilty of worshiping organizational models, doctrines, or traditions instead of the Lord they were established to serve? Have we lost sight of what is most important? It remains an essential step for success in any endeavor, be it sacred or secular, to remember that the most important thing is to keep the most important thing most important. Business guru Steven Covey puts it this way to corporate America, "The Main Thing Is to Keep the Main Thing the Main Thing."[69] Jesus is very specific about what the "main thing" is for the church when he says without compromise, "Seek first the kingdom of God and his righteousness" (Matt. 6:33).

An attempt to answer the question "What is the most important thing for the evangelical church?" is troubling. If we view the focus and activity of the average congregation in contemporary America today, the answer would be "to grow numerically." The decline of many traditional congregations (often referred to as "mainline") and the emergence of the megachurch has created for the average fellowship a mentality of shame unless there is gain in size. For some churches the essential issue has been a doctrinal distinctive (usually one one side or the other of the Calvinist vs. Arminianism doctrine) or a historical tradition (as in Baptist, Methodist, Lutheran, etc.) or a worship style (traditional, charismatic, liturgical, etc.). For others it is a program, a unique ministry or an outright social agenda.

However, as church history demonstrates, doctrines, programs, ministries, or traditions are not enough alone to keep the church vital and relevant. Perhaps the question is better understood if asked in reverse: "What failure to prioritize keeps the church from being what God designed and ordered?" What is it that makes the church the unique vessel through which God

---

[69] Steven Covey, *First Things First* (New York : Simon & Schuster, 1994), 75.

has chosen to reveal his purpose to a fractured world?[70] Is there a singular, essential template through which all facets of the church are to be interpreted and applied? I believe there is and that the answer to that question is a key to bringing healing to wounded congregations as well as to a vibrant, growing fellowship.

The answer, the most important issue to keep important, is grace. Remove grace as the central driving issue for the ekklesia, and you remove Christ from the cross, hope from the gospel, and meaning from the church. The grace by which we are "saved through faith" is the same grace that brings healing to a wounded people, and is the same grace that enlarges and sustains the ekklesia. It seems that too often grace is set aside by prioritizing other issues at the center, or it is hidden away under layers of religious form and functions like the tooth in the Buddhist temple of Sri Lanka. We fail to take it out and look at it daily to remind us of what "the main thing" is all about. The result is we often struggle to find our way through a minefield of religious activities and theological mazes that too often leave more people wounded than rescued.

The Body Language of Grace

Body language is important in any setting. But it is never more important than in a church, especially one in which a congregation is genuine in its desire for God to heal broken fellowship. The *body language* of the ekklesia is always one of grace. The mournful, but meaningful, words of John Newton's simple gospel song, "Amazing Grace," touches deep-seated needs in many hearts. "I once was lost, but now am found, Was blind but now I see" expresses the longing of many souls in search of God.

---

[70] My position is that the church is *the* singular agency of God in the world through which he reveals the mystery of his design and purpose, especially regarding salvation. That is the context of Paul's statement in Ephesians 3:10.

Modern hymnals of traditional congregations have a number of meaningful hymns and gospel songs that extol the meaning and message of grace. Obviously, singing a song is not enough. The poignant question is, do those who are "blind" and "lost" who are seeking it experience grace once inside the walls of the church? For evangelicals, God's grace is the essential element in the experience of personal salvation. For that reason it remains the essential content of the message proclaimed to unbelievers. The "gospel" *is* the "good news" of grace, "For by grace are you saved" (Eph. 2:8). One cannot read the letters of Paul without capturing the significance of *grace* as the crucial essence of the new covenant. For Paul, there is no *antinomian*[71] controversy whereby grace removed any moral standard for behavior. The greatest danger is not that the gospel of grace provides a license to sin but that the message of grace is lost in the human proclivity to depend on a law. The message of Christ is a covenant of grace only, never one of law. To underline how critical the proclamation of grace is to the church, it is worth noting how Paul ended *every* letter with the call to *grace*.[72]

- "The grace of our Lord Jesus be with you" (Romans 16:20).
- "The grace of the Lord Jesus be with you" (1 Corinthians 16:23).
- "May the grace of the Lord Jesus Christ ... be with you all" (2 Corinthians 13:14).
- "The grace of our Lord Jesus Christ be with your spirit" (Galatians 6:18).
- "Grace to all who love our Lord Jesus Christ" (Ephesians 6:24).

---

[71] A label used by Martin Luther for the doctrine that grace removed any need for a moral law.

[72] Except in Hebrews, every letter attributed to Paul also opens with a greeting of grace.

- "The grace of the Lord Jesus Christ be with your spirit" (Philippians 4:23).
- "Grace be with you" (Colossians 4:18).
- "The grace of our Lord Jesus Christ be with you" (1 Thessalonians 5:28).
- "The grace of our Lord Jesus Christ be with you all" (2 Thessalonians 3:18).
- "Grace be with you" (1 Timothy 6:21).
- "Grace be with you" (2 Timothy 4:22).
- "Grace be with you all" (Titus 3:15).
- "The grace of the Lord Jesus Christ be with your spirit" (Philemon 25).
- "Grace be with you all" (Hebrews 13:25).

The preceding list is a summary of what is the "most important." It also emphasizes the true hermeneutic for understanding, not only the gift of God in Christ Jesus, but the nature and body life of the church. Grace describes God's ability on our behalf for eternal salvation as well as our responsibility on behalf of Christ for the life and ministry of his church. The primary and consistent message of the church must be of the grace of God in Christ Jesus. It is grace that must be proclaimed from the pulpit, evidenced in the private lives of members, and demonstrated in the fellowship of the congregation.

Paul's emphasis of grace as the gift of God, and the fundamental agenda for the church, is not without precedent. The incarnation of Jesus was announced as the birth of grace: "The Word became flesh and made his dwelling among us. We have seen his glory, the glory of the One and Only, who came from the Father, full of grace and truth" (John 1:14). Jesus is also the source of grace: "The law was given through Moses; grace and truth came through Jesus Christ" (John 1:17). At Calvary, Jesus became the provision of grace to the whole of the human race: "God's grace and the gift that came by the grace of the one man, Jesus Christ, overflows to the many" (Romans 5:15).

The grace of God in Christ Jesus does not end with the cross. The birth of the church at Pentecost with the gift of the Holy Spirit to every believer, is also the work of grace: "But to each one of us grace has been given as Christ apportioned it" (Ephesians 4:7). The many and diverse expressions of Christ's gift of grace are often understood as gifts of the Spirit, which Paul describes as abilities by which we are empowered to be effective servants in the church.[73] When those gifts are seen as an extension of Christ's grace, the church as the *body of Christ* has a definitive meaning. The arena of grace is the *koinonia* (fellowship) of a local congregation. The interaction of believers responding to one another in accordance with the pattern of Christ's grace creates a redemptive *living body*. Even in this postmodern world, it remains the ultimate practical application of Pentecost. The indwelling Spirit transforms grace from a word that describes God's work of redemption into a living reality. Through the work of the Spirit, the church fulfills God's design and purpose of revealing the "mystery, which for ages past was kept hidden in God" (Ephesians 3:8). It is a revelation that must be modeled and proclaimed in the local church. Grace, as a primary doctrine and a congregational lifestyle, is essential for the renewal of damaged believers, for the healing of wounded congregations, and for welcoming into Christ the stranger who is in search of truth and hope.

Without grace as the critical element for *koinonia*, the church is doomed to an existence of conflict and failure. Without grace as the basis for ministry, the church becomes an organization

---

[73] The listings of gifts of the Spirit in Romans 8, 1 Corinthians 12, and elsewhere are often viewed in terms of the power (or authority) received as some kind of personal identification by believers. It is more productive to the healing of the fellowship to understand personalized abilities/power (*dunamis*) as an opportunity to extend grace in all its meaning and form. Thus, Paul emphasizes that there are diversity of gifts but the same Spirit.

that exists for itself instead of for the work of God. Without grace as a primary attitude toward the world, the church will fail to be the living presence of Christ. When seekers enter a church that does not have a primary focus on grace, sooner or later they will experience the pain of conflict instead of the Spirit of peace. In our world of law and lawlessness (which is a law unto itself), with the inevitable violence and fracturing of the souls of humanity, the church is ordained to be God's vessel of grace for the healing and peace of the wounded multitude. That, perhaps more than any other reason, is why the church is called the "body of Christ." When the message of grace is proclaimed with clarity and the lifestyle of grace is modeled without compromise, an atmosphere of healing permeates the fellowship of believers, and the church becomes a vessel of healing.

How does one define grace, which Jesus incarnated and Paul preached, so that it is received and implemented? Often the problem with a definition is that it becomes formalized and thereby limited, as in a "law of grace." It is the ultimate oxymoron, a radical contradiction, and reflects the difficulty we face in comprehending what grace means. The classic definition of grace, "unmerited favor with God," reflects the impact of the law, which, as Paul argues in his letter to the Romans, exposes our need of salvation while failing miserably to provide a solution. Grace that is understood in terms of filling in one's lack of merit and ability to fulfill the law fails to catch something of the heart of God and distorts grace. Placing a law template over grace leads to cheap grace, the kind that sees oneself as receiving divine forgiveness but failing to comprehend the transforming power of Christ to make a "new creation."[74] It also leads to selfish grace, one that accepts gladly Christ's forgiveness while refusing to view others through that same lens. To joyfully accept God's grace while refusing to

---

[74] "Therefore, if anyone is in Christ, he is a new creation; the old has gone, the new has come!" (2 Corinthians 5:17).

extend grace to others is like shutting off the water to your own garden so none will flow down to the neighbor.

The working definition of grace is expressed in the letters to the churches where the nature of Christ is revealed and believers are encouraged to imitate him in order to conform to his image. It is a grace process of transforming self-centered babies in Christ into mature believers, who serve one another in love. The church at Corinth is a classic example. In the opening greeting of 1 Corinthians, Paul refers to them as "sanctified in Christ Jesus and called to be holy" (1 Corinthians 1:2). Yet the bulk of the letter is about the nongrace attitudes and activities carried on by members that damage individuals, cause divisions in the church, and bring shame on the community. How could they be called "sanctified" and "saints" except by the grace of God in Christ Jesus? It becomes obvious that sainthood is a gift, not a reward. Accordingly, Paul's greeting concludes with the essential words "grace and peace to you."

What follows in 1 Corinthians is an implicit message that the Lord intends for the church to be an extension of that same grace, and that infighting, litigation, jealousy, bickering, immorality, and other nonloving behaviors are happening primarily because they have not learned to live by the covenant of grace. After exposing their spiritual/relational/ecclesiastical failures, Paul then proceeds to teach them how the grace of God in Christ is more than a word for being forgiven. Grace defines the model for the believer's lifestyle and the basis of relationships in the church. But that is only the beginning. Demanding that they exercise grace is one thing; understanding the practical application of grace in the context of community is another. Therefore the remainder of the epistle is a how-to manual for exercising grace. At the heart of that practical section lies the famous "love" chapter of the Bible.[75] It remains the world's best practical definition of grace.

---

[75] See the analysis of 1 Corinthians 13 in chapter 12.

The individual or congregation that uses it as a model for actions and attitudes will experience healing of deep wounds and will be amazed at how life takes on new meaning.

A poignant story from Israel's troubled times is in Nehemiah, beginning with chapter 8. At the dedication of the second temple, the prophet Ezra called the people together to listen to the Word of God. It was a moment time of rediscovery for the Israelites that day. Not only had the nation fallen victim to their enemies but, as captives, had forgotten the secret of their greatness. In their decline, they had retained something of the form of godliness, as expressed in the importance of rebuilding the temple, but they had lost the spiritual reality of being a covenant people. Ezra stood above the congregation that gathered, and when he read the story of their ancestors and of God's covenant of love, they responded with repentance and renewal. The Torah had not been lost so much as they had become lost to the message it revealed.

It seems that a similar situation has befallen the church today. The existence of so many wounded congregations is evidence that we are lost to the meaning of the work of Christ. The theme of grace that permeates every aspect of Jesus as messiah, redeemer, and Lord has given way to a host of alternative themes, many of which are important and seem to be biblical. We try to rebuild the walls of the church, restore its beauty, but it keeps falling down around our religious expectations. The problem is one of sin, not just moral or value sins, but the major sin of hamartia, a wrong focus. We need to be reminded that any issue, doctrine, theology, program, ministry, or activity that displaces the message and practice of grace is "missing the mark." The result is a world of lost souls and an ekklesia of wounded congregations. When grace becomes the *summum bonum* of operation in a body of believers who not only experience it personally in the heart but also express it as the criterion of congregational relationship, then an amazing and blessed healing and renewal begins to unfold in the lives of that fellowship.

With God's grace, the wonderful, exhilarating, liberating process of healing becomes a reality. The proclamation of the gospel of grace *is* the business of the church. For wounded churches, it is the trigger to a healing process toward a miraculous recovery. By facing the need to be a forgiving fellowship through times of introspective waiting on God, coupled with relationship expressions of grace, healing becomes an experienced reality.

CHAPTER 19

The *New* Vision

No one pours new wine into old wineskins. If he does, the wine will
burst the skins, and both the wine and the wineskins will be ruined.
No, he pours new wine into new wineskins.

—Mark 2:22

History and tradition are important to maintain identity.
This is true for national and ethnic groups and is equally so for
congregations. Getting in touch with our roots provides a sense
of belonging and a helpful structure from the past that brings
definition to the present. In order to keep our history and tradition
from becoming an end unto itself, and to use each as part of
God's design and purpose for our lives, it is essential that every
generation recapture the vision of grace so that, like their spiritual
ancestors, they become God's healers.

As we begin the twenty-first century and set our sights on
being the ekklesia in a new millennium, being certain about our
identity and mission has never been more important. Continuing
to be the church of the twentieth century is inadequate. Just
about everything that responded to modernity is wrong for our
postmodern culture. To grasp the vision of ekklesia in the current
age will require a willingness to balance unique, local cultural
history, and tradition with experiences of the new ways and means
of the Spirit.

When we begin to walk in the Spirit, and not in traditions or old paradigms, we discover that He brings a refreshing newness to His people "every morning."[76] When our vision of the church is as God's ordained vessel of grace to the people of our community, a city of refuge and a lighthouse to rescue, it will transform how we go about being the church. This new vision will impact how we view the laity, leaders, and clergy. Further, it will impact how we organize for ministry, how we go about the business of making disciples, and what we do in worship. These are the logical and necessary steps to turn a healed fellowship into a healing vessel. What follows are seven intentional activities that, when acted on by the congregation (pastor and people), can stimulate a new vision for the church resulting in a healing process in the congregation.

Prioritize Servant-Priests

My pastoral journey was mostly with congregations in the northwestern corner of this nation. Those churches were affiliated with the American Baptist Churches of the United States of America (ABCUSA). While these churches are located in what is known as the most unchurched region of the nation and across the continent from the denominational offices in Valley Forge, Pennsylvania, each is deeply influenced with Baptist tradition and history. Baptists may be best known for their emphasis on believers' baptism and the separation of church and state. But there are a couple of other emphases from the Protestant Reformation that provides the backdrop for the Baptist new vision.

"Autonomy of the local congregation" is a deeply rooted Baptist distinctive, reflecting its Congregationalist roots in England as well as in the American colonies. It remains a strong factor today in how the congregation is organized and function. Add to those

---

[76] "Because of the LORD's great love we are not consumed, for his compassions never fail. They are new every morning; great is your faithfulness" (Lamentations 3:22, 23).

factors the reformation tenet of the "priesthood of every believer," and we have the ingredients for either chaos and conflict or congregational unity and effective ministry. If the emphasis is on "autonomy" and "every," as in "individual," then the local body will reflect the American culture of privatized spirituality and self-seeking individualism that can result in congregational chaos. However, if the emphasis is on "congregation" and "priesthood," then a foundation exists for the emergence of a fellowship of servant-priests (i.e., a body of ministers). Tragically, it remains an unfinished business![77]

"A congregation of ministers who are servant-priests" seems to be Paul's intent when he wrote to the church at Ephesus, describing the design and purpose of the believer's gifts of the Spirit "to prepare God's people for works of service, so that the body of Christ may be built up" (Ephesians 4:12). Three functions are identified. One is the responsibility of leaders (pastors) to prepare the people. The people (not the pastor) are to do works of service. The congregation (pastor and people together) are responsible for building up the body of Christ (enlarging the kingdom of grace and love!). Nowhere in Paul's treatise is a hint of self-serving issues, only that of serving others. Serving others for the benefit of their spiritual healing is the work of the servant-priest. Such a concept flies in the face of the entertainment and spectator trend that impacts the contemporary church. Buoyed by the cultural phenomena of sound bites, viewer ratings, and show business, it is easy to understand how performance for spectators has infected the church.[78]

The potential pitfall of the need-driven church is not in developing a contemporary worship form in order to attract people

---

[77] Greg Ogden, *The New Reformation*, (Grand Rapids: Zondervan, 1990), 7.
[78] For an excellent summary of the development of the medium of entertainment in all spheres of our culture, including education and religion, see Neil Postman's *Amusing Ourselves to Death* (New York: Penguin, 1986).

from outside the church. Bringing people into worship is a good thing. While the pursuit of excellence is worthy, the risk is that worship becomes a spectator religion. If seekers come for the show and a blush of spirituality but go away without ever becoming servant-priests, then that church has missed the mark (hamartia).

Of course, that potential folly is not limited to the contemporary church. Traditional fellowships have been in that pit for a long time. It does not take a theological degree to read the Word to understand that there is a critical connection between believing and doing. To accept the covenant gift of grace is to commit to a lifestyle of grace. We are recipients of the grace of God in Christ in order that we might become his minister of grace. How that happens for each individual will likely be unique. My own process is described below. I share it to emphasize the importance of being called by the Spirit to ministry to emphasize that in we all are called to serve in some way.

Recognize the Call to Ministry

When I accepted Christ at the age of twelve, many of the adults in my home church slapped me on the back and exclaimed, "Isn't it great that you are going into the ministry!" It was something I had never said, but when they kept repeating it, I assumed that it was true. Years later, as a pastor struggling with the destructive habits of a wounded congregation, I seriously questioned that call. For the first decade of my work in the church, I wondered, "Was I called by God or pushed by men?"

I now know that the answer is by both. I was called of God to minister, and I was encouraged, if not pushed, by well-meaning people to become a pastor. In discovering my calling on both counts, two important truths became self-evident. First, is the realization that not everyone is called to pastoral ministry—but I was and some people saw that before I did. Second, while not everyone is called to be a pastor, everyone in Christ is called to be a minister, a servant-priest. It is a brilliant bit of God's design and purpose. The priestly ministry of helping people experience the grace of God, and of providing ways and means for the development of Christ-like character in their lives, is a ministry given to *every believer*. Emphasis is on the words *every believer*.

When at Pentecost, the Spirit of God was poured out upon all (men and women, young and old), the restricted priesthood disappeared, to no longer exist. It died with the law, when Jesus was nailed to the cross.[79] A new priesthood was instituted in place of the Leviticus priesthood. It is called "the church." That is why Peter could write to those isolated, persecuted, and scattered believers, "You are a chosen people, a royal priesthood, a holy nation, a people belonging to God, that you may declare the praises of him who called you out of darkness into his wonderful light" (1 Peter 2:9).

Remove Labels ("Laity" and "Clergy")

A major step toward the healing of a wounded congregation is to change the paradigm of how the people (*laos* or *laity*) perceive themselves as players and not spectators. Some churches print on their worship folders: *Ministers—the congregation*. Printing it in the worship folder may be a step in the right direction;however, there has to be a practical implementation in place to give substance to the statement. It is an extremely difficult paradigm for a congregation to embrace, for it requires doing away with the perceptive differences that separate clergy from laity, a challenging activity but necessary outcome. It means that the clergy must let go of their entitlement to the ivory tower, abandon the use of language forms that set their education and theological

---

[79] "When you were dead in your sins and in the uncircumcision of your sinful nature, God made you alive with Christ. He forgave us all our sins, having cancelled the written code, with its regulations, that was against us and that stood opposed to us; he took it away, nailing it to the cross" (Colossians 2:13, 14).

understanding apart, and afford the congregation the opportunity to participate in worship and ministry functions that have traditionally been reserved for clergy.

At stake, for some, will be the opening up of sacred duties, such as serving of communion, baptism, and so on, to the people. That is a challenge for liturgical and sacramental traditions that have a long history of clergy representing the "sacred" and the laity representing the "common," thus preventing them from performing sacred functions. It also challenges nontraditional fellowships, like Baptist, who have developed an unofficial hierarchy in which only a few (usually men) are allowed to serve communion. As I challenged a deacon board in a church, I have yet to find in scripture why only a man and not a woman qualifies for that ministry. To the opposite intent, Paul makes it clear in Galatians 3:28 that in the ekklesia there is no gender distinction.[80] For healing to be real so that the church models complete grace in a world of prejudice and conflict, it is essential that the Old Testament institution of the priesthood becomes a "peoplehood" of the new covenant.[81]

Learn to Listen to God

When the members of a congregation are empowered to see their roles as ministers, it has a major impact on them in two ways. One is how they learn to apply the grace activity of understanding other people (chapter 14). This demands the skill of intentional listening. Successful business and corporate people know that one of the secrets to their success is the ability to listen to others. Any worthwhile book or workshop on self-improvement and management techniques has a section on developing listening skills. They all teach that the key is to stop judging what you think

---

[80] "There is neither Jew nor Greek, slave nor free, male nor female, for you are all one in Christ Jesus" (Galatians 3:28).
[81] Ogden, 19.

the other person is saying, while formulating what you are going to say to correct them when it's your turn. Instead, just listen. Listen with the intent to discern where they are coming from, how they think and why, what their real needs are, how they have been scripted, what their fears, worries, or hidden wounds may be. It is called "empathetic listening," with a goal of understanding for the singular purpose of responding in love.

Several listening skills mark the grace-filled congregation. The first one has to do with maintaining the source of grace, which is learning to listen to God. It is not just about learning meditation techniques, although that is an appropriate style of personal devotion to be pursued. More important than technique is the reason for seeking God. Listening to God is a spiritual exercise for the primary reason of discerning His will. The most common reason for prayer, and probably the most nonprofitable, are our prayers that tell God what we want, what He should do, and how to do it. These prayers often result in a self-centered expectation of God's response, instead of a Christ-centered response to God's purposes. Not only does it result in times of seemingly silence from God or in emotions of being disappointed with God (an incredibly stupid idea!), but also it prevents one from discovering God's will wherein there is utmost meaning and joy.

The spiritual discipline of listening to God is a root issue for the heart of every individual and a critical exercise for a congregation in order to experience healing. It is in the heart, where one decides whether to be a person of violence and discord or a priest of grace and unity. In the same way, it is in the corporate prayer and listening exercise that a people decide to be a congregation of consuming spectators or servant–priests. In the human heart, the will of God is rejected or accepted, and where either the wickedness of man's inhumanity to man or Christ's grace and love to others is determined.[82] Learning to listen to God with a desire to know and to do His will is critical to individuals being priests of grace and to congregations becoming safe harbors of peace and healing.

Learn to Listen to Each Other

There is a parallel listening skill, an extension of the heart that seeks to hear the voice of God. It, too, is a learned spiritual discipline. It is the willingness to listen to another person with a desire to hear their soul and heart. The mandate to "love one another" is an exercise of grace precisely because it requires us to hear without judgment on each other's stories, which, if honestly communicated, reveal the pains, fears, and hopes that drive us onward as well as hinder our abilities to be open and vulnerable. Learning to listen is to be willing to look beyond the appearance, behavior, or trait that is irritating or repulsive, and to see the battered and scarred soul in search of healing. It is to feel the pain, to share the shame, and to glimpse the windows through which life is viewed. This kind of listening grace impacts a congregation of servant-ministers. Understanding gives way to sympathy, empathy, and compassion so that, instead of complaint, gossip, prejudice, and rejection, there is confession, acceptance, and healing.

When a congregation trusts God enough to listen to one another, the forces that cause pain, conflict, rejection, and accusation are replaced with the spirit of grace, love, and peace. The door is open for a new kind of believer to step forward in the life of the healing fellowship. Created in the inner sanctum of God's preexistent design, and modeled after the Savior, the *servant-priest* emerges. Not every member will respond. For some the whole idea sounds like a fantasy some muddle-minded

---

[82] Thomas Torrance, *The Mediation of Christ* (Colorado Springs: Helmers & Howard, 1992), 31.

preacher conjured up. But the truth is the congregation that overcomes the disaster of conflict and division always have some servant-priests who emerge. These individuals have caught the vision of the ekklesia, are impacted by the plight and need of people who are without Christ, and discover the secret of serving as the avenue to a life of meaning and joy. It is incongruous to experience grace and not become involved in the life of the church.

Create a Servant-Friendly Environment

While not everyone will step over the line from consumer to producer, many will if given the opportunity. Two things have to happen to make involvement a reality for most people. One is to create a servant-friendly environment. It begins with recognizing everyone involved in activities of grace as servant ministers, not just those who sing, teach, preach, or lead. Holding to the standard Paul gave the church at Corinth, while there are many different gifts and ministries, every one is equally important to the whole of the body. Not only are all spiritual gifts important, but also all their functions are essential to the whole. To neglect or belittle is not only a violation of love and grace but also can lead to congregational suicide. Every church needs to find ways, within their tradition and forms, to recognize and honor all servant-priests.

Of course there are some risks involved in doing so publicly. Those left out of being recognized may end up with hurt feelings. The fact that someone feels forgotten underlines the need to recognize and honor *all* servants. Another risk is that some may feel that their exercise as a servant is a private and sacred issue, and that public acclaim is not appropriate. Being discerning and sensitive is necessary. The point is that creative ways of bringing honor to all servants needs to be developed. In any case, the benefits a congregation receives from recognizing all servants are greater than the risks.

A greater challenge for recovering churches is for servant-priests to recognize that serving is a calling not a duty. A duty can become a burden, as obligation replaces desire, and can lead to burnout. A calling is a gift in which exercising that gift is one of pleasure and satisfaction. Like nothing else, exercising your gift can bring meaning and fulfillment. A common complaint of church leaders is that people will not take on responsibility. Christian education directors are constantly scrambling for teachers and nominating committees use all kinds of ploys to fill the slate of candidates for office. Later, they bemoan the number of nonfunctioning members on boards and committees. At the same time other members drop out because they know they are not fulfilled a particular endeavor. Often it is a bad fit that does the opposite of helping to heal a wounded congregation.

Match Spiritual Gifts with Servant Opportunities

There is a common scenario in the many churches that reveals the need for renewal of the vision of servant-priests. At its heart, it reflects a loss of a biblically defined grace issue: be sure individuals who serve are also called, and be sure they are gifted by the Spirit to serve where they are called. In reactive language, never fill a position with a body. In proactive language: always give a servant-priest an opportunity to fulfill his or her calling. It usually is better to leave a position open, even to close a ministry program, than to twist some unwilling member's arm to serve as its leader. The reason for the unwillingness may be a lack of commitment, but it may also be spiritual wisdom of understanding personal giftedness and calling.

The world of business carries the motto that "form follows function." But in the kingdom of Christ, the motto is, "Function follows gifting." That is the nature of the body described in 1 Corinthians 12. After listing a number of different spiritual gifts, Paul makes the point: "All these are the work of one and the same

Spirit, and he gives them to each one, just as he determines" (verse 11). He then points out the importance of each and every part: "The body is a unit, though it is made up of many parts; and though all its parts are many, they form one body. So it is with Christ. Now the body is not made up of one part but of many. If the foot should say, "Because I am not a hand, I do not belong to the body," it would not for that reason cease to be part of the body. And if the ear should say, "Because I am not an eye, I do not belong to the body," it would not for that reason cease to be part of the body. If the whole body were an eye, where would the sense of hearing be? If the whole body were an ear, where would the sense of smell be? But in fact God has arranged the parts in the body, every one of them, just as he wanted them to be. If they were all one part, where would the body be?" (verses12, 14–19).

Who of us knows better than the Spirit about these things? True, the absence of a gifted, willing servant may mean that a position will go empty or a ministry will struggle or be closed. So be it! Equally true is the fact that there will be an absence of nonvisionary people, who often either misfire personally and create conflict, simply because they are not functioning under the direction of the Spirit. Just as important as filling a position is the fulfillment of a servant-priest who is matched with the right opportunity for ministry. Again, it is a combination pregnant with the power of grace.

When people understand their spiritual gifts as a blessed opportunity, good things happen. The servant-priest experiences a fulfillment in serving that becomes its own reward without any public recognition. We are, I believe, the happiest, most fulfilled, and spiritually alive we can ever be when we are living as servant-priest in the power of the Spirit. It is then that spiritual grace becomes the living reality of lifestyle and the source of spiritual, emotional and relational fulfillment. It is impossible to mature in Christ without exercising personal gifts of grace. When the people of a congregation become servant-priests and begin to work in harmony with one another, a noticeable excellence begins to characterize that fellowship. The ministry of grace heals a congregation when it empowers those servant-priests to listen to God, to each other, and to those in the community. That kind of grace listening results in a healthy church as the members experience the meaning and joy of serving. It also becomes the template for restructuring the organizational model of a church to support a grace-designed ministry.

CHAPTER 20

Ministry Design

If anyone wants to be first, he must be the
very last, and the servant of all.
—Mark 9:35

A *Wizard of Id* cartoon has the king in his lofty tower looking
down on the peasants gathered below. He shouts to them,
"Remember the Golden Rule." One of the peasants asks "What
is that?" The king responds "He who has the gold makes all the
rules." We live in a world (not just our culture) that worships at
the altar of power. In the marketplace, in the corporate world, in
politics and in sports, those in positions of authority have more
power. It is no wonder, therefore, that one of the most common
forms of hamartia in the church today is the abuse of power.
Whether it be gatekeepers who determine who is in and who is
out, or a pastor who feels the need to maintain control and uses the
position of his office to demand authority, the exercise of power
inevitably destroys the community of grace.[83]

There are many rationalizations for seeking power in the
church. Often the use of theological statements and creeds are
screens for power as statements of faith are exercised in order to
keep the church pure by keeping impure people out. It is a sham,

---

[83] Arlin J. Rothauge, *Sizing Up a Congregation* (New York: Seabury), 11.

a manipulation of God for personal control, for if the scriptures were really being sought for direction, a contrite and repentant heart would ensue, with a commitment to serve and empower others rather than control them.

Controlling the finances by a few elites in the church is another common exercise of power. The ability of the congregation to carry out its ministries is maintained by a Judas mentality. One of the common rationalizations for control by an elite power group is for the church to be more efficient and less cumbersome in its operations. For that reason, there is a trend in some evangelical circles to return to elder- or deacon-run churches, wherein a small group exercises their will on everything including pastoral choice, how the church worships, what ministries are implemented, and who is either included or excluded from the fellowship. Some pastors see their positions as heads of the local congregation, or at least of the local board of elders or deacons who run the church. Some churches expect that kind of headship of the pastor.

It would be wrong to suggest that churches that operate on a power-pyramid organizational form do not succeed. Some of the oldest and largest denominations have traditionally operated on that system. The Roman Catholic church is a prime example, as well as the Church of England and others. However, success in the world does not necessarily mean that it is what was intended by Christ. While churches so structured may function with some degree of success, the idea of a head with power that controls every facet of the church is a perverted view of the meaning of head as defined in the scriptures and demonstrated by Christ. A historic expression of that error is the gender bias that is based on three passages of scripture that describe man as *head* of woman in the same way that Christ is head of the church and God is head of Christ (1 Corinthians 11:3, Ephesians 5:23, and Colossians 1:18). If we take an Old Testament view of headship, which was a judicial/hierarchical authority given to male, human leaders, then headship indeed equates to authority and power. We can then rightfully conclude that God has established a pyramid order of power for the church and the home. It is logical for those who so perceive of a "divine order of authority" to extend that paradigm to the community as well, insisting that civil authorities fall under the God's ordained religious power pyramid.

However, is that the meaning of head and headship in the new covenant of grace? A study of the New Testament usage of the word *head* reveals a different paradigm. Of the seventy-five occurrences of "head" (*kephale*) in the New Testament, most are a reference to someone's physical head. A few are references to Christ as the *head cornerstone* and *head of the church*. None are used to denote position of authority and power with control over others. Instead, they are about relationship. Authority, with its power to control and demand obedience, as in a superior/inferior position, is not suggested or implied. Instead of leadership of the power/authority design, headship in the covenant of grace is leadership of the surrender/sacrificial kind.

That is the explicit message of Ephesians 5:21–33. The banner flying over the entire passage is vs. 21: "Submit to one another out of reverence for Christ." The example of *Christ as head of the church* (v. 25), is not one of chain of command but of submission. The cross is the place of ultimate submission and surrender where the Savior dies on her (the church's) behalf, making her holy through the sacrificial gift of grace. This image is so radically opposite to the idea of authority, superiority, command, and control that it is difficult to express. Instead of a paradigm of power, the model for the church is the image of surrender, sacrifice, serving, and empowering, all important reflections of grace.[84]

The idea of headship as power and authority does not come from the voice and will of God, but reflects the pattern of our world. I think it is repugnant to the Holy One, a blasphemy in the

---

[84] Lawrence O. Richards and Clyde Hoeldtke, *A Theology of Church Leadership* (Grand Rapids: Zondervan, 1981), 15–26.

church! The only way headship can be translated as authority of leadership is to use the Greek culture as a template through which the scriptures are selectively read. The impact of Alexander the Great's saturating his world with Hellenistic thought and his own credo of power remains the dominant paradigm for that world. That is why the way of grace is "foolishness to the Greeks" (1 Corinthians 1:23). In contrast, to grasp and comprehend that the power of God one must consider the death of Jesus. As Newbigin so succinctly puts it, "The king reigns from the tree."[85] The power of sacrificial redemption is incomprehensible apart from the paradigm of grace. If the church abdicates to the worldly domain and continues to operate according to a paradigm of power instead of grace, seeking to accomplish the kingdom of God through ruling instead of by serving, then the sight, sound, and aroma of grace will be lost in the stench of conflict and division.

Including the congregation in the design and implementation of the church's ministry becomes another crucial step in the healing process and in the renewal of the ekklesia. The issue is not one of ownership but of partnership. When a people submit to the will of God and are dedicated to using their unique spiritual gifts together in the church, then relevant program design will emerge. Ministry forms will be developed around needs in the congregation and in the community. The result will have many blessings. Congregants will experience spiritual growth and fulfillment through serving. People, in the church and in the community, will experience the touch of God through the works of that church. And the church will experience a joy and celebration as they sense the presence of God. It can only happen that way when the congregation is empowered to be the church. It is difficult for task-oriented leaders (and pastors) to be patient with such a process, especially when the congregation has been

---

[85] Lesslie Newbigin, *Foolishness to the Greeks* (Grand Rapids,: Eerdmans, 1990), 99.

subjected to numerous organizational and planning models that are so deeply scripted by a timetable mentality for success. But when the congregation catches the vision and become the formulators and implementers of ministry, grace begins to be the way of life of the community in the church.

The preceding is the basis of the leadership and congregational planning process of a healing and ultimately healthy church. Planning process and ministry design is the responsibility of both the congregation and leadership. Often a model of research and idea gathering is implemented by leadership and carried to the congregation for broader input. On other occasions, the initial input is at the congregational level and then given to the leadership for refinement of the process. The final result, in either case, is a unity-based decision because the church is intentionally seeking the will of God over the plans of man.

Essential for the success of a servant-priest ministry is trust in God to fulfill His will through both the process and through one another. The need for effective communication cuts across every facet of the church life and remains the Achilles' heel of unity in any congregation. The need to hear and be heard requires constant work at clearing away the obstacles of miscommunication, replacing them with better methods, tools, and practices. Miscommunication is a problem for wounded churches just as it is in broken relationships. The issues that divide are really by-products of our inabilities or unwillingness to do the work of listening, understanding, and being understood. Detecting those areas of conflict, which are the result of noncommunication, and devising strategies to open the lines of dialogue becomes an important work of grace.

Often, causes of communication difficulty are obvious because they are systemic and mechanical. The very structures and traditions of the fellowship create a variety of communication blocks that, in turn, can result in conflict. Organizational styles can set up a turf mentality or a superior/inferior model. The abuse of power and a culture of distrust and suspicion of motives is too often built into the organizational model. When that happens, conflict will often develop as those with power become domineering. In some instances, those without authority will practice guerrilla sabotage. It is not that the players are necessarily evil people, but they have a bad model in which to work. Human nature being what it is, warfare and protection of turf occurs. Language often reveals a win/lose attitude as different departments speak in terms of "us" versus "them." The vision of a shared mission and common ministry becomes buried under a wreckage of tug-of-war, often over insignificant issues.

One church I pastored suffered from this malaise. The membership were victims of an inefficient and unworkable infrastructure that was set up a century ago, and although it had become a problem instead of a problem-solver, it had become tradition. To a certain degree, the perspectives, turf alignments to be protected, and types of battles fought became a tradition as well. Trustees did not trust deacons, and vice versa. Suspicion and assumptions regarding motives were a common response, making trust and love impossible. One church board refused to take meeting minutes because they did not want the other boards to know what had been discussed. Obviously, there was little or no communication between the boards. Church business meetings were often a battlefield, as motions were made and argued that would sway power one way or another. All that was needed was a pastor who would become a third party, and the fuse was ignited for a major explosion. Tragically, it went boom!

Reading through the church constitution and bylaws revealed that the stage for a major conflict was built into the organizational model. The congregation was led by five boards, each responsible for an area of church life and each with a portion of the church budget under their control. The church was thereby divided into five competing elements with nothing to maintain a sense of the whole, except perhaps the pastor. Another problem was that they had a reputation of being hard on pastors, as most lasted only for about three and a half years before leaving either angry, frustrated, or ashamed.

The strategy for bringing grace and healing to this organizational monster was in two parts. The first part is much easier and less dangerous to accomplish than the second part. To establish open communications and begin the renewal of a shared vision, three immediate recommendations were made, readily accepted, and implemented. The first was to have the boards meet at the same time on the same night. The evening would begin with a brief scripture and prayer led by the pastor, with a focus on the design and purpose of God for the church. Unity, shared vision, common mission, and connecting to other servants who were on boards was a vital part of that agenda. By meeting on the same night, concerns that involved more than one board could be covered at a joint meeting for part of the evening. The pastor and moderator moved from board to board, sharing information, carrying communications, and encouraging common vision.

The second recommendation had to do with written communication by the boards. Every board and committee was asked to submit to the church secretary a copy of the minutes of the meeting just held. She then made multiple copies of the minutes, getting a copy to every member of every board as well as posting them on a bulletin board dedicated to that purpose. No secret meetings or confidential minutes were allowed.

The third recommendation was to establish a coordinating council composed of the chairperson of each of the boards, plus the moderator, clerk, and pastor. The purpose of this leadership group was to provide a forum for communication of concerns, issues, and agendas that are current in the boards, and to set the church calendar for the next month. While it had no real power, it provided a genuine sense of common vision and paved the way for acceptance of a new model, which was the organization reform needed for improved communications.

The task of redesigning the entire model of how to be a church where the format empowered the congregation to function as an agency of grace and healing was difficult and carried a certain amount of risk. That was because it triggered the second cause of ineffective communication: wrong assumptions and unrealistic expectations. The old church joke that the seven last words of the church are "We never did it that way before" is not funny when it comes to altering the forms and formulas that have been in place forever. Habits are difficult to change, even when they involve insignificant outcomes. When it is a habit of a religious type, change can be very volatile. Development of an agreed upon strategy is essential. If leadership and the congregation buy into a plan, then change can be expected.

There are some good models that can be copied, although I do recommend finding a highly competent facilitator who can lead the congregation through a careful process of evaluation, discovery and planning. As a new design for carrying out the ministry vision (new wineskin) emerges, it should be shared with the congregation so that there is unity for the final result. Every church that sets forth to recreate their operational model according to a bottom-up, servant model of grace should be aware that it will be difficult to communicate and implement. That is because the community at large is deeply scripted in a top-down, power model of organization that dominates virtually every aspect of life But for the church, God's agency of grace, the motivation and design must reflect the bottom-up, servant model Jesus established.

On this rock I will build my church, and the
gates of Hades will not overcome it.
—Matthew 16:18 NIV

CHAPTER 21

No-Fault Infrastructure

He is the one who gave these gifts to the church: the apostles, the
prophets, the evangelists, and the pastors and teachers. Their
responsibility is to equip God's people to do his work and build
up the church, the body of Christ, until we come to such unity in
our faith and knowledge of God's Son that we will be mature
and full grown in the Lord, measuring
up to the full stature of Christ.
—Ephesians 4:11–13 NLT

Organize To Empower Ministries

Organizational infrastructure must always be seen as a means to
a certain end, not the end in itself. To paraphrase Jesus's statement
in Mark 2:27 that "the Sabbath was made for man, not man for
the Sabbath," organizations exist for persons and not persons
for programs.[86] It is important, therefore, for administrators,
whether they be pastor or lay leadership, to operate on the
principles of grace with the goal of healing and empowering in
mind. Just as it is necessary for organizational design to enhance
communication rather than cause conflict, it is essential that the
structure of administration be committed to an empowering of

---

[86] Alvin J. Lindgren, *Foundations for Purposeful Church Administration*
(Nashville: Abingdon, 1990).

the congregation for ministry. The nature of grace is always to empower, support, and liberate. In contrast, the nature of a power and authority structure is to control and blame.

An important strategy to empower the laity is to separate function from form by how the church's organization/ administration documents are written. The legal and formal definition (constitution) should be limited to answering "what?" It will include such information as to the church's purpose, affiliation, beliefs, membership, and its format for organization. The goal should be to create a "form" document that provides a solid foundation for structure without having to be modified every time the ways and means of the church are altered. When both form and function are combined, then each time a new trend impacts the church in how it fulfills her mission, the documents (form) often rules instead of empowers. The options left for the congregation are to force new wine into old wineskins, which can eventually cause disaster, or to ignore the format that is established in the form documents and operate in violation of them, a decision that can in time, create conflict. Inevitably, when tensions arise, there may be an accusation by some who call for "legal righteousness." The option, then, is to go through the difficult, and sometimes controversial, process of changing the foundation document to fit the new ministry form. Of course, if the church survives and thrives, future generations will have to go through the same process because times change and so do ways of doing ministry, even though the mission and purpose remains the same.

However, when the functions of the congregation, the "how," are defined in an adjunct form, such as a policy manual, then flexibility for ministry empowers and provides opportunity for people to do the work of ministry to which they are called. The *function document* should include such information as staffing policy and standards, job descriptions (for every position, committee, board, etc.), organizational structure with ministry descriptions and relationships, worship, education, and missions policy, membership expectations and process, and so on. Information that provides guidance, direction, and structure to various ministries of the fellowship, and in so doing gives form to communication and relationship, should be included in the *functions manual*. It must also contain succinct and clear directions for congregational procedures for changing the document—via a simple process—as ministry forms and directions change. Those procedures should be, in effect, feasible, for as servant-priests are empowered to do ministry, and as listening and responding takes place in the context of grace, changes in function, and in types of ministries, will occur.

Redefining the Expectations of the Professional Staff

Empowering and liberating professional staff may be more difficult than doing so for the laity. The unrealistic and overwhelming expectations of professional clergy is documented in many books and articles today. Burnout is a word used to describe the fast fall experienced by many, and the numbers of clergy casualties are cause for much concern. According to reliable sources, we will soon face a shortage of qualified and capable senior ministers in churches.[87] The reasons given for a clergy shortfall range from a concern that many seminaries are still training for the "congregations of the past" and that increasing numbers of ministry candidates are opting for counseling, or some other form of ministry, in order to avoid the difficulty of pastoral ministry. Some leadership authors claim that being a senior pastor is one of the most difficult professional positions in America today. These writers equate the responsibilities with college president sans similar pay or perks!

If healing is the objective and grace is the means, then the principles of calling and function must apply to the professional

---

[87] Leith Anderson, 79.

staff as well. It is crucial that staff are allowed and empowered to be servant-priests according to their giftings and calls. What happens so often is that the expectations of staff, combined with a desire to succeed, causes them to be given several areas of ministry to which they are expected to give expert leadership. If their area of spiritual gift is in one of those areas of responsibility, one of two things often will happen: the staff member will be focused on the area of giftedness to the neglect of the others, or he or she will attempt to make the other areas of responsibility successful while the one area of giftedness experiences mediocrity. Ordaining men and women into ministry and then expecting them to achieve more than is possible based on time and resources or to do what they are not gifted for is to build guaranteed failure into the church's design for success.

The dilemma for the average church is that there is not enough money to hire a staff person for every ministry emphasis, especially considering the increasing cost of maintaining full-time staff. A redefining of the expectations of professional staff in conjunction with the grace paradigm of an empowered laity provides a model for solving the staff dilemma. It also frees up funds for missions and new ministries that would normally be used to provide staffing.

One way to develop a new strategy for staffing is to begin with if-then statements. If expectations of professional staff are too great, and leads to burnout or conflict or both in the church, then expectations need to be changed to be realistic. If the cost of maintaining enough professional staff keeps the church from funding missions and new ministries, then additional sources of financial resources need to be developed and more efficient ways for staffing the church need to implemented. If we really believe in the "congregation as the ministers" standard of grace, then it is essential to empower the laity to do more ministry.

The following proposal, which formulated a strategy for staffing with a view to fiscal efficiency and ministry excellence, was made to one congregation I served. It was proposed: "That the ministry staffing needs of this fellowship be fulfilled by several individuals (ministry coordinators) who are to be given responsibility for a specific ministry and to be paid on a part-time basis accordingly." It was presented as an intentional alternative to the model of hiring full-time professional staff and supported by a document giving the rationale and process. To adopt the proposal meant that the congregation would seek to fulfill its mission through the use of limited responsibility/paid-ministry coordinators rather than through the full-time associate-pastor model. This new model supported the concept of the congregation as ministers, as the opportunity to be a ministry coordinator would be open to laity and clergy alike. Ministry responsibility was to be based on ability and spiritual gifts so that optimum effectiveness is possible.

Often there are trained people in the congregation with precisely the skills (grace gifts) needed who do not want to work full time but who do want to find a place of ministry. To avoid burnout and unwarranted expectations, ministry coordinators are discouraged from being involved in any other aspect of the church's overall ministry. Reimbursement is to be limited with pay according to the time and responsibility expectations of that ministry. This allows the church to use the cost of one full-time associate pastor to provide for at least five or six effective ministry coordinators.

Each ministry coordinator is to function as a pastoral staff member by providing support to a specific board, and has a primary relationship with that board as well as with the pastor. The responsibilities for their particular arena of ministry includes program design, development of resources, recruitment and training of volunteer workers, and oversight of ministry activities. No other assignments or expectations are given, except as agreed to by the pastor, board chair, and coordinator, and as reimbursed accordingly. This staffing plan achieves greater effectiveness of paid staff and allows more flexibility for ministry needs in that additional staff can be added with a minimum impact on the budget.

The congregation, in an unusual mood for change, agreed unanimously to the proposal. Four initial areas of staffing need were immediately identified and prioritized according to the ministry vision at that time. Within a year, three of the four were filled from within the congregation by individuals who were both gifted and professionally trained. In each case those individuals had been praying for an opportunity for ministry. The need for other ministry coordinators on the horizon could be added according to the need and the emergence of qualified and called individuals.

Create a Climate of Cooperation

The phrase "Christians in conflict" should be viewed as an oxymoron. Unfortunately, too often it describes what is happening within the congregational life of many churches. On the other hand, the idea of Christians dealing with problems is not only acceptable but also a sign of grace at work. The difference between conflict and problems is significant. H. Newton Maloney identifies conflict as that which goes on inside our heads and reflects ego involvement, fears, and distress, whereas problems are about disputes and differences of opinion.[88] It is important for church leaders and members to learn ways to reduce conflict and to solve problems. Equally important is the development of a strategy designed to create a climate of continuing cooperation within the congregation.

The climate of cooperation begins with leadership and is a critical issue for the pastor, who must exercise the principles of grace in all relationships. The principles include forgiving and

[88] H. Newton Maloney, *When Getting Along Seems Impossible* (Old Tappan: Fleming H. Revell, 1989), 31.

asking for forgiveness, honesty and transparency, sensitivity to others, listening and seeking to understand, and trusting God for means and outcomes rather than insistence on having his or her own way. If those in leadership do not model daily cooperation, conflict will surely overcome the fellowship.

A strategy to create a climate where cooperation flourishes involves both the physical and organizational innovations enumerated above. Creating a plurality of communication means and activities, designing the organizational and management model for interaction and information, using meetings, sermons, and business meetings to foster a shared vision, and incorporating the congregation into the planning as well as the process, are some of those ways discussed earlier.

Other methods of creating a climate of cooperation are not so easily manifested, but are equally important. Learning to detect when someone is going into conflict, and pursuing them with a definite process to detect and defuse are critical skills for both pastors and lay leaders.[89] Learning skills and language that reveal love instead of anger for the one who is in conflict require personal development through reading, study, and practice. Through all these processes and learned skills lies the important priority of grace. That is, the daily awareness that the church is to be a place of healing, never of wounding. When conflict becomes the norm, instead of cooperation, it is a sign of deep spiritual problems.

The environment of cooperation begins with truly caring for people and making them feel welcome. Many churches print "welcome" on their literature, state it in pulpit announcements, and then proceed to make it clear that unless you believe a certain narrow biblical interpretation, have experienced certain mystical moments, or are morally and spiritually pure, you will not be comfortable in this congregation. It is a challenge for many fellowships to confront the reality of people's fractured and often

---

[89] Ibid, 173.

failed lives, and to accept them into worship without passing judgment.

Yet that is where the rubber of grace meets the road of sin. It is important to differentiate between being welcomed into worship (the arena of grace), accepting into membership, or being placed in a leadership role, but the bottom line for all levels of involvement remains the same—grace. We do not keep the church pure by assuring that everyone who enters the door is pure. The holiness of the church is dependent entirely upon the grace of God in Christ Jesus. We keep the church authentically the body of Christ by creating a climate of healing and wholeness. Cooperation depends largely upon the willingness of the members to live by grace and not by law. If there is to be any error on this point, be sure to err on the side of grace!

Remove Gender- and Position-Discrimination Practices

Many books have been written on the topics of gender bias and racial discrimination practices. Books do not solve the problem, for it is fundamentally an issue of the heart. How can servant-priests, who have been recreated in the image of Christ and are driven by grace, consider another human inadequate for certain spiritual activities, just because that person isn't the right gender? How can the people for whom Jesus was nailed on the cross be considered unworthy of fellowship or restricted from ministry for the primary reason of their skin color? Where does the gospel of grace even suggest that a history of immorality—especially sexual immorality—disqualifies that person from ministry forever? It does not!

The gospel of grace is about regeneration, renewal, and restoration. It thrives on forgiveness, transformation and inclusion. Grace is the one power that can break down the walls of separation.[90] It is an affront to the King who rules from the tree to exclude or debase those for whom he died. Every time we exercise gender, race, nationality, or pious discrimination, we are pounding the nails into his flesh, demanding that the evil of our hearts that judge others as less than self rules supreme. Of all human institutions, organizations, and fellowships, the church of Jesus Christ should be the most open, most gracious, most free of any practices or forms of discrimination. Instead, it appears to be one of the last fortresses of the bigotry that plagues our world. When prejudice is gone, who will we blame for our problems?

This is a crucial issue but one filled with ecclesiastical land mines. A strategy to remove this evil from the arena of grace must be carefully devised and prayerfully implemented. The first priority is to remember that grace is the rule. However, it is not effective, and is less than gracious, to confront head on long-standing prejudices and, in so doing, destroy what unity of the fellowship presently exists. To do so would make that issue more important than the ministry of healing.

Patience and grace must become the rule for understanding the deep-rooted biases of others, while not approving of them. It is important to view those who practice discrimination in the same way we see sin still at work in all lives. We must recognize that although they are struggling with sin, they are in Christ and, therefore, objects of his grace. Because the issue is deeply spiritual, the strategy needs to be long term and spiritual. Through prayer and trusting in God's timing, there will be opportunities to break down the causes of such discrimination. Fear, tradition, and a crisis in biblical literacy are at the root of such beliefs, along with a refusal to submit to God's will. When a formal institution or practice of

---

[90] In Ephesians 2:14 Paul describes the work of Christ in terms of the removal of the walls in the temple which prevented gentiles and women from entering into the main worship area. "For he himself is our peace, who has made the two one and has destroyed the barrier, the dividing wall of hostility."

the church falls along such lines, the challenge will be to find alternative ways of doing things so that discriminatory practices are changed. This, then, becomes an avenue to demonstrate grace while the development of a new paradigm emerges.

An illustration of instituting change without confrontation occurred in one of my churches when Communion was moved to a Sunday evening once a quarter. When the invitation was given for anyone who felt called to serve, an equal number of women and men responded—without a single complaint coming across my desk. From that simple act, the walls of gender discrimination began to crumble. A deacon confided in me that he had long felt that women should not be allowed to serve or lead men, but now felt okay about it being done. He learned the importance of evaluating his prior rational and began searching the Bible for truth. This is the spirit of change at work.

The Spirit of Christ was poured out upon all at Pentecost without discrimination as to gender, age, race or nationality. Peter's quotation of the prophet's words removed age and gender distinctions in the church,[91] and the response by two thousand pilgrims from many nations and creeds wiped out any kind of race, nationality, or other form of exclusion. In establishing churches, Paul echoed that same kind of inclusion. Any doubt regarding the inclusive nature of the body of Christ should be removed by his pronouncement of Galatians 3:28: "There is neither Jew nor Greek, slave nor free, male nor female, for you are all one in Christ Jesus." The renewal of the church today into an arena of grace where healing of wounded souls can take place, demands that we continue to chip away, everywhere, at all forms of bigotry.

---

[91] Acts 2: 17–18: "God says, I will pour out my Spirit on all people. Your sons and daughters will prophesy, your young men will see visions, your old men will dream dreams. Even on my servants, both men and women, I will pour out my Spirit in those days, and they will prophesy."

CHAPTER 22

Ministries that Heal

I in them and you in me. May they be brought to
complete unity to let the world know that you sent me
and have loved them even as you have loved me.
—John 17:23

That day in the hill country of the Philistines when a shepherd boy stepped forward to battle the obscene, shouting Goliath, he was presented with many obstacles. Before he could get onto the battlefield of conflict with the foul-mouthed behemoth of fear, he had to sidestep some land mines in his own camp. The stereotyping by his family, a scripting that could have prevented him from even trying to fulfill his calling, resulted in and verbal abuse by his brothers. Their accusations were obvious projections of their own fears and pride. Sidestepping around that by playing to the fears of a reluctant leader, King Saul, he gained acceptance of his call to fight giants, only to be confronted with an even greater threat to his ability to succeed—a traditional program.

Fighting the enemy was done by using specific tools while wearing the standard-issue protective equipment. The "program" meant that the shepherd boy would wear armor—the king's armor—and do battle with a sword—the king's sword. Had David staggered out to meet Goliath under the load of that "program," no doubt history would read differently today. David's survival and his opportunity for success depended upon his setting aside the prescribed "program" to operate on a different basis. His purpose was not to follow a "program," but to carry out a specific mission.

Rejecting the official fighting equipment of the day, he took that with which he was most familiar and skilled: a staff, five smooth stones, and slingshot. The story remains one of the favorites of all time. Everyone, perhaps with the exception of giants and bullies, rejoice when the underdog wins. An interesting twist to the story is that after knocking down the giant with a stone from his unorthodox weapon, he took the "program" weapon of the day, Goliath's sword, and, with it, severed the Philistine's head.[92] This popular biblical story demonstrates what happens when the "program" becomes more important than the mission. When that happens, then the program can become an Achilles' heel and be the cause of demise.

As noted before, the expression that the seven last words of the church are "we've never done it that way before" is usually said with a smile. A play on the seven last words of Christ, It is cynical humor, for it is a painful reminder that in the church we easily fall into the hamartia of substituting program for mission. Even when the language of workshops and seminars on church renewal are about meaning and mission, the understanding gets translated into form, so that "how" something is done becomes the agenda. The result is that many of the forms used in growing churches become program models that struggling (and often wounded) churches adopt in the hope of experiencing renewal. Perhaps that is because it is easier to understand and implement a program than it is to discern and prioritize our mission through Spirit-empowered ministries. A church program carries the idea of a fixed form, with certain parameters being maintained in order to make the program succeed. As such, it develops a program

---

[92] The account of David's defeat of the Philistine, Goliath is recorded in 1 Samuel 17.

centered emphasis. A ministry, on the other hand, is mission centered and remains flexible so that the needs of people are effectively related to the healing power of Jesus Christ. Therefore, it is important for a theology of healing to emphasize ministry rather than focus on programs.

The four areas of ministry focus listed below are more philosophical than mechanical, representing some major arenas of ministry that are important in bringing healing to a wounded fellowship. How they are developed into programmatic form and congregational habit is avoided. Form and style will vary, dependent upon a variety of factors, such as the gifts and style of the pastor, the history, traditions, and expectations of the people, and the felt needs of the community. The goal of each form mentioned below is to enhance the healing of the fellowship first of all, and secondly, to empower the body of believers to become a healing community.

Blended Worship

Many astute students of the contemporary church observe that one of the major dividing issues of congregational style is music. Contemporary Americans consistently rank music slightly above preaching as the important factor to their spiritual growth.[93] That is not surprising considering the impact music has in our culture. It is aided by a continually improving technology to give us multiple listening tools in our homes, offices, vehicles, and recreational equipment. Music has become a far more pervasive aspect of life than almost anything else in our daily routine. That is indicated by the fact that in 1961 there were only fifteen gold records awarded for selling a million copies, but in 1991 that number had grown to 217.[94]

---

[93] Herb Miller, *Connecting with God* (Nashville: Abingdon Press, 1994), 47–48.

[94] "Database," *US News & World Report*, February 17, 1992, p. 10. quoted by Herb Miller in *Connecting with God*, 48.

It should come as no surprise that music has become a major issue of controversy and division in the church. People often look for a church that play "my kind of music." Because our music preferences are formed in our teen and young-adult years, it usually means different generations want different kinds of music.[95] The Boomers, who grew up with the Beatles and a variety of rock-and-roll music inspired by Elvis Pressley, prefer that style of music, accompanied with synthesizers and electric guitars. It is no surprise that many of them find little connection to music written in the medieval centuries played in stately form on a piano or organ.

Conversely, those born before World War II often find limited spiritual connection with praise songs of contemporary worship. The result has been the emergence of the "generational church," with the dividing factor being music. Of course there is more to the difference between the generations than music.[96] However, because of the importance music plays in corporate worship, and due to weekly worship service being the dominant church involvement for most people, music has become a major trigger issue. Thus, the medium that was intended to provide an atmosphere for the Spirit to unite a congregation in worship has often become, instead, a source of hostility and division. How it must sadden the heart of God, for whenever the church is divided, whether it be along generation, economic, gender, or racial lines, it loses its ability to be a healing fellowship.

In the same way a single parent cannot be both mother and father to children, resulting in disadvantages that can create social/relational problems in their adult life, a single-generation church cannot provide important elements of fellowship needed to create an atmosphere of healing. The need for mentoring of young believers through spiritual counsel by their elders is prevented in a congregation void of gray hair. Likewise, the energy, vitality and

---

[95] Ibid.

[96] Gary L. McIntosh, "What's in a Name?," *Church Growth Network* (May, 1991).

new persectives along with the support and assistance provided by young parents to elder generations is an invaluable benefit for those who participate in a multigenerational congregation. Benefits flow both ways. The delight that children and youth bring to older generations, and the interaction with younger generations in social as well as worship events, create in the elders a feeling of love and satisfaction. To establish and promote churches that are generationally limited is being shortsighted. In the long run, such emphasis will add to the wounding of congregations, and the very tool (music) that was used to create success will end up being that which leads to its downfall.

Given the trend toward divided worship styles, how does a congregation meet the needs and satisfy the preferences of the divergent groups of worshippers that have developed along generational lines? One way is to ignore trends and continue to do what has been the long-standing tradition, especially in terms of music and message. To do so is to become one of the growing number of declining congregations, as members gravitate toward churches that are more "contemporary" in worship style. Often referred to as "mainline" churches, being limited to a specific liturgy and being controlled by a "builder" generation, it will mean that there will be little understanding of the likes and needs of the contemporary generations with little accommodation of their preferences.

There *is* an argument that can be made for holding the line on traditional worship forms. While not often heard, it raises serious questions from a biblical perspective. Questions should be asked about the intentional nature of the contemporary church to take its signals from the world's ways and means. The emphasis of spiritual principles through drama, and a worship form that revolves around contemporary music forms, reflect the culture instead of the biblical agenda, which is to proclaim Christ through the foolishness of preaching[97] and to worship with inspired music

---

[97] 1 Corinthians 1:21.

that reflects both Christian theology and history. The argument is that in an age in which everything else is impacted by the trends and values of a fragmented and polarized society, it is essential that the church maintain a unique identity where escape from present-day culture into a spiritual enclave is possible.

However, to defend that position is to assume that the traditional forms are exclusive and relevant and that new forms cannot maintain a biblical emphasis. Such an assumption is to risk making the mistake of limiting God and avoiding the ever-changing application of the gospel. The unavoidable reality of such thinking is that of mistaking a "program" for "ministry" so that the very thing that is clutched with such tenacity becomes the sword by which the head is severed from the body. The bottom line is that churches that refuse to change will die. William Easum believes that their deaths are permitted by God, who doesn't care about program or tradition but "cares if they meet the spiritual needs of those God sends their way."[98] The challenge to be relevant in ministry demands a focus with flexibility, including the music mix that goes into worship.

Changing the music in a worship service not only has an immediate impact on an existing congregation, but also reflects the community of believers a church is seeking to serve. The fastest growing churches, in numbers, are often those that target the baby boomer generation. Such churches often make the radical move of replacing hymns with praise songs, hymnals with overhead screens, organs/pianos with electronic synthesizers, and choirs with worship teams. The beat is lively, and the volume higher than in traditional services. It creates a feeling of excitement, and provides an emotional response that, to many, is synonymous with "real worship."

Seminars are held around the nation, teaching pastors and worship leaders how to become a growing church with a celebratory worship. By implementing principles from the

---

[98] Easum, *Dancing with Dinosaurs*, 15.

advertising industry, and designing worship experiences from an entertainment perspective, "church" is redesigned to appeal to a generation that had been noticeably missing. The Church Growth Institute flyer, advertising seminars to be held in 1996, demonstrates the vastness of the generational gaps that exist, and that can dominate a congregation's life. In it they list the differences of *Worship … Then & Now.*[99]

THEN	NOW
Hymns	Praise songs
Organ/piano	Small band
Hymn books	Overheads/slides
Song leader	Worship leader
Slower pacing	Faster pacing
Quietness	Talking
Softer sounds	Louder sounds
Longer service	Shorter service
Sermon	Message
Standard format	Variable format
Bulletin	Worship folder
Soft lighting	Bright lighting
Contemplative atmosphere	Celebrative atmosphere
Choir	Praise team
Content-oriented	Heart-oriented
Sanctuary	Auditorium
Audio orientation	Visual orientation
Varied talent used	Best talent used
Haphazard service	Rehearsed service
Little planning	Much planning

[99] "Designing a Worship Service to Reach the Unchurched, " *Church Growth Institute* (1996).

As numerous growing fellowships reveal, it is an effective way to numerical growth and to reach certain targeted groups of people. Unfortunately, like the traditional-music-only church, the one-sided style of music and worship results in generations missing from the fellowship. In both cases, the ability of the body of believers to experience the fullness of fellowship in an environment that is enhanced by all generations is limited at best, and most likely negligible.

My intent is not to critique either worship style or suggest that their content and purpose is void of the Spirit. However, it is my intention to suggest that there is an alternative that provides the basis for congregations to respond to a wide range of worship needs, and in so doing preserve the fellowship as a family of generations who understand and seek to serve one another. Consistent with the theological position stated at the beginning of this book, a healing fellowship will develop a blended worship style. A blended worship style provides a variety of music and worship forms that not only meet the felt needs of different generations but also teach the value of each. For example, some of the great hymns of faith are theology put to classic music and express the attributes and works of God. God is both the subject and the object, as expressions of His nature, love and deeds are anthems of praise and adoration. Such hymns provide fundamental doctrine and theology and enhance the process of making disciples.

In contrast, at the other end of the spectrum, many of the gospel songs and popular praise music are expressions of personal experience, with testimonies of the power of God at work in the life of the individual. This music often includes praise to Jesus or an invitation to the Spirit to move in their midst, but both the subject and the object is often self, as evidenced by personal pronouns "I" and "me." There is a vast amount of music between these two forms that combine both theology and testimony. To do away with hymns is a mistake that must not be made in the church, for it robs new people of the great theology and history of the church. In the same way, to reject praise music as shallow and without substance is to deny the community of believers the often emotional Spirit-empowered witness of faith. Not only for sake of generational balance in the congregation, but for the sake of worship balance in the individual, a blended philosophy of worship is preferred.

Each congregation has to determine the form a blended worship will take. In most blended worship services there is a combination of hymns and praise songs. The selection of specific songs, as well as the order in which they are sung, is determined by the theme of the service and the goal of the music. The most common format is to open the worship time with upbeat praise songs and hymns in combination, along a theme, and move toward a devotional hymn or praise song that sets the mood for prayer. However, there are times when a worship service may be given entirely to one format or another. On occasion the service can be designed along a more formal, almost liturgical, style with responsive readings, the Lord's prayer, and hymns sung in a more quiet manner. On other occasions the design can be more celebrative in style, with praise singing and choruses, drama, and a time for congregational praying. The result is a blended fellowship in which there is little complaint about the music, and many comments about being blessed by the blended and diverse style. It has been said that to blend the two styles results in everybody being unhappy. If that is true then there is a deeper spiritual issue at work. The bottom line is that a blended worship style is a visible statement that all generations are welcome and that this congregation is committed to a ministry of healing.

Ministry-Focused Cells Based on Needs of Specific Groups

The church growth movement has shown that one of the most successful ways to evangelize and to grow is through small groups. There are many forms of this ministry being carried out in the church today. Some of the best-known churches in America have been built around the small-group format. In my opinion, the best argument for the validity of the megachurch is the inclusion of people in Bible study groups. If the "lite gospel" in a drama-and-praise format is what people receive on Sunday, it is not adequate to grow strong disciples. By introducing them into a small group, several important dynamics of nurture takes place. The fundamental need to become familiar with biblical content and the meaning of the message it contains (knowledge of the person and work of Christ) can be fulfilled through the small group dynamic. Beyond that, the development of a trust group that creates a confidential and supportive environment provides reality to the meaning of fellowship. In such group dynamics the seed of grace will be nurtured and enlarged through the process of prayer with love and genuine care. Small groups can provide a viable framework to carry out a healing ministry to the fragmented and frantic lifestyles of today's family.

In a healing fellowship, an effective small-group ministry seems to have the greatest impact when the groups are organized around the needs, interests, or desires of the participants. Some needs can be assumed for all groups, such as the need for a deeper understanding of the Word, for spiritual growth, and for a broader experience of the grace and mercy of God. When a small group is organized around a specific need factor, then other needs, especially those that are related to wounds, scars, and baggage of life, are shared within the group according to individual circumstances. These are often referred to as "felt needs" and represent a wide spectrum of mutual identities such as addiction recovery, parenting, marriage, divorce, victim healing, and so on. The focus of such groups is determined by the people present in the fellowship.

Not all groups are organized around "felt needs." Other groups are often primarily Bible study and spiritual growth groups. These will often develop according to different phases of life that provide similar needs and experiences. Singles, young married, young mothers, parenting, empty nesters, retired, and so on are indicative of the kinds of common-interest groups who pursue Bible study. As in the case of felt-need groups, these small groups will likely become primary places of accountability, encouragement, and social interaction. The confidential nature of discussion will become an important element in the healing process for individuals, as the group becomes an intimate fellowship where confidences can be held, prayers can be specific, and grace is exercised. Healed individuals combine to create a healthy, healing fellowship.

A third kind of group in the healing fellowship falls under the category of special-interest groups. Individuals are drawn together, not because of felt need, or primarily for Bible study, but because of a common interest or function. Music groups, activity groups, recreational groups, mission groups, drama troupes, athletic teams, coffee clutches, and others provide a major form of group dynamic. The list of such cells is endless, and by understanding them as important in the life of the congregation, they provide a cutting edge element to the renewal of the church. Who can see far enough into the future to predetermine what interest areas will be fermenting in society in a decade or two? When special interest groups are perceived as having a spiritual dynamic, then there is opportunity for them to become prayer and care support cells as well as vehicles for evangelism.

Anderson writes, "The message that must be kept before all types of groups is that they are a form of ministry. That means that the group is not the end in itself, and that the group exists to provide an extension of the larger fellowship."[100] If the group becomes an end in itself, it has become ingrown, which can lead to a fragmentation of the larger fellowship, creating division instead of unity. Where there is no unity, there will be no healing. The purpose of all groups is to provide a vehicle for the administration of grace in order to bring healing to individual lives. The is the essence of Paul's definition of the purpose of ministry in Ephesians 4:12–13: "to prepare God's people for works of service, so that the body of Christ may be built up until we all reach unity in the faith and in the knowledge of the Son of God and become mature, attaining to the whole measure of the fullness of Christ." Groups that reflect this model will develop a sense of ministry through serving.

Teach Inside-Out Lifestyle

The challenge of the apostle Paul in Romans 12:2, to "be transformed," implies a promise as well as a challenge. The implication is that we can experience real and evidential transformation through the faith in Jesus Christ. Such a conclusion is consistent with the teachings of Jesus and is a common theme in the letters to the churches.

It is not surprising that the hope of a transformed life upon acceptance of Christ as Savior is a common promise of evangelistic preaching. Many individuals exercise genuine faith in response to the gospel, desiring personal change and believing that their conversion will somehow mystically result in a new person. But soon they discover that the "wretched" condition described in

---

[100] Leith Anderson, pp 62–64, lists four kinds of groups found in the growing churches: discipleship groups, covenant groups, support and recovery groups, and cell-based groups. He believes that the most biblical and effective is the cell-based group, which meets "all of the basic spiritual needs of the people" and are "not part of the paradigm community; they are the paradigm community." In cell-based groups "*everything* exists for the cells, is operated by the cells and strengthens the life of the cells."

Romans 7 is at work in their lives, driving them to violate their own desire for holiness.[101] Unfortunately, many conclude that they were not really saved, or worse yet, that the claims of Christ are a cruel joke. For many others, it is a life of accepting the fact that they fall far short, that they are trapped by habits and desires that run counter to their desire to serve God. Grace becomes their ticket to heaven, but guilt and shame become their companion in daily living. They go through life feeling unworthy, wondering why God will not change them.

Sermons and Bible studies that hold up the model of the ideal Christian only serve to enhance their senses of failure. Verses, such as "Therefore, if anyone is in Christ, he is a new creation; the old has gone, the new has come!" (2 Corinthians. 5:17) are either passed over or interpreted as having spiritual meaning but no practical relevance. The result is that many believers do not experience the healing impact Jesus intended. The vast horde of nontransformed believers are both cause and victims of brokenness in the church

The power of the gospel to transform individuals through the healing of the entire person is one of the best-kept secrets of the day. Perhaps it is a forgotten process in the church, with doctrinal debates and social issues having pushed it to the backburner of concern. Because it is a strategic and important element of personal growth and maturity, it is being revived today, only not by the messengers of grace, but by the psychologists of business management and New Age gurus. It is a process that belongs to the church, and it must be revived as a primary tool for making disciples. Essential to bringing the gospel of grace into the lives of individuals so that they experience the transforming power of Christ as a healing dynamic is to prioritize the *inside-out process.*

---

[101] Paul decries the fact that no matter how hard he tries in his own strength to effect holiness, he fails because he is trapped in the flesh. His self-definition as that of a "wretched man" describes any person who seeks to be holy outside of reliance on the grace of Christ.

Transformation begins in the core of the individuals personality, that mystical place where the will is formulated. Jesus called it the "heart" of man, while the apostle Paul often referred to it as the "mind." It is important to note that his implied promise of "being transformed" in Romans 12:2 also gives the secret to experiencing authentic change for the better. It is "by the renewing of the *mind*."

To the atheistic naturalist, the mind is synonymous with the matter that constitutes the brain cells. It is a contradiction of the empirical standard, for the definition of the mind merely in terms of matter and electrical impulses fails to explain the phenomena of creativity that occurs. The ability to develop a language, and communicate with other humans so that meaning is conveyed, cannot be explained by naturalists.[102] The naturalist's definition of the brain fails to account for the intellect, which is defined by language, cognitive skills (imagining something that does not exist and then creating it), and the exercising of a will. It is that creativity ability that dramatically separates humanity from all other life forms. Emotions, desires, and priorities all are born in the heart of man. Jesus described the way the heart works by saying that it is where good and evil behavior and attitudes are produced.[103]

The *inside-out* process begins with defining, or understanding, what is at the center and then building priorities, values, and a life mission out from that center. For the Christian it begins with the awareness that Christ is the center. The heart of the believer is a "new heart," washed by Christ's blood, infused with the Holy Spirit, and born anew. Believing that, and experiencing the

---

[102] Mortimer J. Adler, *Intellect* (New York: MacMillian Publishing House, 1990), 126–133.

[103] Matthew 15:19–20: "For out of the heart come evil thoughts, murder, adultery, sexual immorality, theft, false testimony, slander. These are what make a man 'unclean.'"

transformation implied, requires an intentional activity of the mind.

Many people believe in Jesus as their Savior. It is a confession of their need of his forgiving grace, and a dependency on his righteousness for hope of eternal life. However, to make Jesus my Lord requires a mental process that becomes an act of my will in which there is a determination to make all of my life a response to his indwelling Spirit. It is a major spiritual step, for to decide to make Jesus the Lord requires the setting aside of personal desires and agenda. This is an act of self-denial and a "taking up the cross."

It is never easy to deny oneself, and requires a willful choice that can only be exercised by the individual. That is why the biggest obstacle to our spiritual growth is the self-centered will, which is defined in the scriptures as "pride." Pride rules in our hearts naturally, and will continue to do so unless we exercise that intentional act of enthroning Christ.

It needs to be understood that the center of self is manifested in many forms. Any focus that drives a life, other than the cross of Christ, is ultimately a self-centered program. We give ourselves to such causes as a way of feeling good about who we are. Some of those common alternative centers are represented by whatever our time, money, and energy are used for: family, spouse, children, church, work or profession, money, pleasure, etc.[104] Making a conscious decision to set self aside and put Christ at the center of who we are is to align our personal centers with our professions of faith and with the promise of God. Christ is at the center of the life, on the throne of the heart, and in position to effect transformation in that life. Given that intentional choice, there is,

---

[104] Covey, pp. 118–121. He lists a number of alternative centers which afflict us, showing some of the causes and results. His argument is to develop a "character" center as opposed to being "personality" centered. Self-centered is shown as one of the many instead of as the root of all alternative centers.

then, a basis upon which to rebuild one's life according to one's Christ-centered heart.

Once the issue of center is settled, it then becomes important to do inside-out thinking: "If Christ is the center of my life, then what are the principles that will guide my life?" Principles are truths that transcend any individual, common denominators that cannot be lost or altered. Principles are points of our inner compass that provide the wisdom necessary to live a Christ-centered life. Accordingly, any principles that are adopted and owned by an individual will be guiding truths that are compatible with, and an extension of, the nature of Jesus Christ.

There may be some room for individuality of principles, dependent upon personality, culture and understanding of the church. It will be important that they are principles that are related to Christ, and not a program of the self. However, because of the person and work of Christ, there are some principles that are essential to being a follower of Christ, and will be owned by everyone who operates on an inside-out spiritual process.

Christ"s principle of *faith* is to acknowledge that one is dependent on God, without proof, and it becomes the motivation for a life based on his fulfilling his promises. *Grace* is the fundamental principle of Christ's life acted out in all of his relationships. Claiming God's unearned favor will give birth to values that impact life such as *forgiveness* and *mercy*. The principle of *love* will imitate Christ's response to the wounds and needs of individuals. When an individual owns love as a guiding principle of life, then judging others will be replaced with seeking to understand them. Excluding others because of their race, gender, and other superficial characteristics will be transformed into a heart of inclusion as serving replaces judging. *Truth* must surely become a guiding principle too, for the one whose heart is centered on Christ will seek to live with character values of integrity, honesty and stewardship. The adoption of *hope* as a guiding principle empowers the believer to transcend the nominal issues of daily life while being reminded of its greater meaning and purpose.

When an individual defines his or her principles for life as expressions of a Christ-centered heart, a harmonizing of the human will with the will of God becomes a reality. The renewing of the mind has resulted in a transformation of the heart so that there is conformation to the image of Christ. Throughout his ministry, Jesus announced that the driving focus of his heart was to do his Father's will, to be obedient and submissive to the divine design and purpose. A conviction is implied, that we are the happiest, most complete and contented we can ever be when we are living out of that divine center and seeking to be obedient to the will of God. For the individual, it is a conviction that is experienced in the process of living from the inside out.

The determination of personal values is a necessary next outcome of the inside-out process. Values are guidelines for action that empower the believer to fulfill the Christ-centered principles in the heat of the battle of life. Like principles, values reflect the center of one's life, although they are practical guidelines based upon a principle. For example, if an individual has decided that grace is a principle that will imitate Christ, and therefore predetermine personal responses in life's daily issues, then a value of that principle will be forgiveness. To forgive those who have violated you, whether it be direct or indirect action, is an expression of the grace whereby we are forgiven by Christ. It is a value that, when acted out in interpersonal relationships, results in tremendous personal benefits while giving support to other important values.[105]

Love, another important principle for any serious believer, will also lead to the expression of other critical values for daily living. A value such as communication will express love by "seeking first to understand, then to be understood," as discussed in chapter 2.

---

[105] See chapter 3.

That same love principle will result in a value of serving others as a guide for daily activities.

Values based upon principles will at first be learned responses. That is because our natural self-center immediately reacts negatively to perceived violations of our will and person. Learning to respond in love, instead of reacting, moves the inside-out process of transformation from theory to reality. Being proactive instead of reactive is a critical issue. *Reactive* means that whenever something happens that threatens or violates your space, agenda or will, you act accordingly to what has transpired. Reactive people allow the external elements and events of life to dictate the agenda for their life. A person who reacts to an injustice by harboring the pain, being "hurt" until some kind of punitive damages are paid, is in bondage to that injustice. His or her emotions, and spiritual wellness, are continually impacted by bitterness and resentment that hang on like a ball and chain.

For the reactionary person, all causes and remedies are external. Reactionaries not only focus on the external enemy, their hope for resolving the pain is for some external messiah to "make it right." It is a false hope and longing, for the real Messiah has established his kingdom in our hearts.[106] That is why the law failed. It was an external obligation, while faith is the beginning of the internal (inside-out) solution. Whenever we expect some outside source or person to provide our peace and joy, be it government, pastors, or families, we are subject to constant wounding and disappointment. The solution is not "out there," but inside the soul, where the heart that is focused on Christ is empowered by the Holy Spirit to develop a personal set of principles and values that when put into practice, begin the process of healing and wholeness.

---

[106] Luke 17:20–21 Once, having been asked by the Pharisees when the kingdom of God would come, Jesus replied, "The kingdom of God does not come with your careful observation, nor will people say, 'Here it is,' or 'There it is,' because the kingdom of God is within you."

Instead of being reactive, the healthy (wounded, but healing) individual develops the proactive lifestyle. By the inside-out process, when the angst of life occurs, the Christ-centered believer chooses to respond according to the inner working of the Spirit of God. The question "What would Christ do?" has a quicker and more valid response. Rooted in the Christ-centered principles of the heart, a value is acted out with confidence in the rightness of the action. Proactive believers are driven not by external persons or objects, but by internal principles and the Spirit of Christ. The result is that individuals not only experience the wonder of being transformed by Christ, and in so doing experience a wide range of personal healing, but also become agents of healing who are eager to fulfill the divine design and purpose of their redemption.

The inside-out dynamic is not only for wounded believers but also for bringing healing to wounded congregations. It is important for a church body to affirm that Christ is the very center of their fellowship and that the cross of Christ symbolizes their mission and defines their method. The process of bringing a wounded people to healing begins with a constant reminder that the focus of faith is Jesus Christ, and not personalities, music, buildings, or anything else. When the Christ of Calvary becomes the heart of the church, the process of recapturing the principles of being the body of Christ is the next critical step to wholeness. Then, in the power of the Spirit, these divine principles—these holy characteristics of the church (faith, grace, love, hope, truth, etc.)—will be translated into congregational values that give definition to ministries that not only lead to healing but also transform the church into God's agency of healing.

Celebrate at Every Opportunity

When congregational life revolves around the person and work of Christ, and the dynamic of healing is happening through the inside-out process, the fruit of the Spirit becomes a constant phenomenon. Joy begins to be the common expression of congregational life. Just as laughter is a healing phenomena of the human body, celebration is a demonstration of healing in the spiritual body. It is, therefore, important to use every opportunity available to celebrate.

In one church I pastored, special events became opportunities to celebrate. A fellowship time following morning worship was established, providing a setting and opportunity for joy to be expressed. While it is common practice in many churches, it had the feeling of something new and provided a place for healing and renewal to take place. The celebrative nature of the fellowship time was enhanced by the recognition of birthdays on the last Sunday of each month. On those days a birthday cake was served in addition to the usual coffee and punch. Another important form of celebration was to focus on anniversary dates of the life of the congregation. We had a hundred-year party celebrating the arrival of the missionaries in a chapel car five years before the church had been established. That triggered a major celebration for the centennial of the official beginning of the church. Church picnics were reinstituted, with games and activities for all ages. Special occasions, potlucks, and seasonal events (Thanksgiving, Christmas, etc.) were joyful moments of congregational life.

These kinds of celebration are important to the sense of joy that will pervade the congregation. Yet it is in the framework of worship that the ultimate celebration experience takes place.

The joy of celebrating life through baby dedications should given special attention. It provides an opportunity to highlight not only the importance of family but also the essential role the congregation has in support of parents in the task of raising the child with an understanding of God. Part of that responsibility is in the modeling of a congregational lifestyle of joy and unity.

The ordinance of baptism is an important moment of joy for the congregation ion worship as believers follow the Lord through the waters that symbolize submission to the will of God. There is a keen awareness that it is both a congregational and a personal experience, as the reason for that individual's coming to Christ often is because of the witness of one or more of the members. Observance of the Lord's table is a quiet moment of congregational celebration. Recognizing the body of the Lord is to be made aware of the broader encompass of God's grace. Again, it is a reminder of both a personal and a congregational experience. Music, though, remains a major vehicle of celebration. To sing psalms, hymns, and spiritual songs with gratitude in our hearts to God (Colossians 3:16) is to experience the Spirit of joy in community. That is precisely as it should be, for joy is one of the ultimate marks of the believer who has experienced the healing power of God and who is set on the course of a ministry of healing. What better demonstration to a watching world that the Messiah is among us than the evidence of joy. This is the expressed desire of Jesus for his people: "I have told you this so that my joy may be in you and that your joy may be complete," (John 15:11). When healing defines the life of a congregation, the Messiah is truly among us!

CHAPTER 23

A View from the Pulpit

But you are a chosen people, a royal priesthood, a holy nation,
a people belonging to God, that you may declare the praises of him
who called you out of darkness into his wonderful light.
—1 Peter 2:9

It Is Halftime

It was too painful to watch, so I turned off the television and went
to the office to prepare for the evening service. Greg Norman,
the number-one golfer in the world, had begun the final day of
the Masters Tournament with a six-stroke lead, the largest in
that tournament's history. By the time it was over he would lose
by five strokes. It will probably always be remembered as the
tournament Norman lost. The question that will continually be
asked is "What happened?" Perhaps the most viable explanation
is that he made the mistake of playing to protect the lead instead
of playing to win the tournament. So many athletic teams have
gone into the locker room at halftime of a game with a big lead,
only to lose in the second half. Instead of continuing to do what
had brought them success, they felt comfortable with the lead and
settled down to maintain the status quo.

Protecting the status quo is a mental/spiritual attitude that
poses a threat to all healthy congregations. When a wounded

fellowship experiences spiritual and relational healing as a result of intentional application of Christ-centered values of love, grace, and mercy, numerical growth is often the result. It is an inside-out process. The emphasis is on spiritual growth. Yet true to the pattern of the Holy Spirit, as a result of spiritual regeneration, renewal, and restoration of individuals, there is an increase in numbers of believers in the fellowship.[107] Wounded people from the outside enter into the corporate warmth of the congregation, experience a healing environment, and then stay. Worship services become full, and the various elements of worship grow in quality and effectiveness. In some ways it is a dangerous time. When the combination of worship experiences, educational opportunities, and fellowship activities create a feeling of being "comfortable," it is only natural to want to keep things that way. It is a Mount of Transfiguration kind of experience with a desire to capture the experience because "it feels so good."[108] When a wounded congregation has experienced the healing process and has come to a place of wholeness and fulfillment, it is easy to develop a mentality akin to a team going to the locker room at halftime with a sizable lead in the game. While there is legitimate reason to feel good about the "wholeness" of the congregation, it is a critical moment in the life of that fellowship.

The focus on spiritual formation at the beginning of renewal resulted in numerous members becoming involved in acts of love, compassion, and grace. On a daily basis such acts are committed, mostly out of sight of the majority and without any expectation of recognition. That activity of love is paralleled with an absence of

---

[107] On the day of Pentecost (Acts 2) the direct result of the ministry of the Holy Spirit was the confession of faith and baptizing of three thousand new converts, "which were added to their number that day" (Acts 2:41). It was a pattern that would be repeated throughout the book of Acts.

[108] The Synoptic Gospels all record the event of Jesus's transfiguration at which Moses and Elijah appeared. Peter suggested the building of three shelters for them, a natural human reaction to keep exceptional moments from passing.

conflict in the midst of a variety of individual styles, perspectives and needs. There has been a growing army of kingdom servants who gave of their time, energy, and resources for ministry to others as a way of serving the Lord Jesus Christ. Prayer marks the fellowship in many forms and events, with a confidence in God who listens and answers.

A genuine and warm welcome is extended to visitors and becomes a mark of the fellowship. Indicative of this new openness was a memorial service held for Gene, a man in just such a church. He was brought to church initially by one of the retired couples who made a habit of ministering to people in need. A recovered alcoholic, Gene was unable to work and existed without material possessions. He was not only welcomed but also was befriended by many in the church. His coming into the life of the church was as if God wanted him to experience a touch of grace while still in this world.

Then the house in which he rented a room burned to the ground. He escaped the fire by jumping out a second-story window. Complaining of back pain a few days later, after his escape, he visited a doctor and was diagnosed with cancer. Gene died within two weeks of the diagnosis. Having been long rejected by his family, his only caregivers had been members of the church. Its memorial service in Gene's memory was a symbol of the transformation that had taken place. Instead of just being a wounded congregation, it had become a spiritual, healing fellowship.

It is halftime. We have the lead, "things are looking good," victory is in sight. The question is, will we make the common mistake of only living and serving to protect the lead? It is a critical time in the life of the congregation, a crossroads that will determine the future of the fellowship for years to come. Congregations often arrive at such a moment, and either do not sense the importance of it, or do not have sufficient faith to respond positively to the new vision. The temptation is to play it safe, be comfortable, work to protect the status quo, and play not to lose instead of playing to win.

Questions that often confront a healed congregation are

- How important is growth?
- Do we want to grow?
- Do we want to move to the next level, both in terms of numbers of people attending and new ministries implemented?
- Or, do we want to keep things the way they are as to routing, comfortable, painless, while pleasantly upbeat?

Virtually every congregation of course will answer "Yes!" to those questions. However, they are superficial questions, for they do not get to the heart of the issue. A critical following question is, will we pay the price for growth? The price is not just the financial expense that growth requires. In a sense the greater price is the loss of a comfortable community of believers in which we know and are known. To respond with vision and ministry will result in more people, more children, additional staff, facility expansion, and larger budgets. Changes in the size and ministry of the congregation will necessitate changes in the organization and in the role of pastors, leaders and members.

If the answer by the congregation continues to be yes, then the most important questions become

- Will we catch the vision?
- Will we be willing to look deeply into the eyes and hearts of the people who live in this community, see the needs, the wounds, feel where there is brokenness, and respond with compassion and mercy?
- Will you let your heart be broken for those whose lives are fractured?

- Will we commit to a mission of being a sanctuary of peace and a vessel of healing for people who are victims in this world?

Ultimately, the question of vision is not about growth but about ministry. Being a congregation that has experienced both the *emptiness* of division and the fullness of God's grace in healing is not enough.[109] We are healed by Christ *for* the purpose of becoming the healing presence of Christ. The critical next step for a wounded, now healed congregation is to capture a larger vision for itself to become a healing ministry.

New Ministries for Old Wounds

What kind of a church we will be in the future will be determined by what kind of programs give direction to the church or what kind of ministries emerge out of the fellowship. The intent of a healthy church should be to develop ministries rather than design programs.

The difference is significant. When a program is developed it becomes the structure to which people are required to conform. A ministry is the opposite. Both wounded and healed people are the reality and a ministry is a response to both immediate and long-term needs met with the gospel of grace. Ministries that heal will involve at least three elements: the need identified, the response clarified, and the resource verified.

Beginning by identifying the needs of people, instead of identifying the program to which we are committed, will result in flexible forms of ministry. Need identification means that the members of the church will turn from focusing on internal healing to seeing the needs in a community of broken lives, dysfunctional homes, destroyed relationships, and deeply wounded individuals.

---

[109] Ray Anderson, *God So Loved: A Theology for Ministry Formation* (Huntington Beach: Privately printed, 1995), 41–43.

The commitment will move from a self-focused spiritual journey to a deep concern for helping hurting people.

How churches can gather information and translate it into ministries that heal could be the subject of another book. Churches exist that have accomplished this purpose and continue to do so. The terrain of culture and people constantly changes in many ways, while remaining the same in others. What will never change is that each generation experiences life in a unique way, and in so doing, suffers wounds to the heart and soul, to self-esteem, hopes and dreams. Relationships, family connections, and physical lives are damaged and wounded. The only constant in lives such as these is the never-ending, always healing, and ever-present grace of God in Christ Jesus.

We can help people in many ways and respond to their many human and emotional needs. But the greatest gift we will ever give another person is the vision of Christ and the message of His love and compassion The eternal fact is that this vision has been placed in the custody of local churches. Too often churches use their facility and function as an art museum, a piece to be admired but not touched. Others use it as a corporate mission, a motivation to rise higher and be known as superior to others, and others use their church as a concert hall or a hospital, a place to go to to feel better about themselves. But the fellowship that survives the arrows of the enemy of God, endures the division and destruction that follows, and experiences the marvelous grace of God in Christ and His healing touch, that fellowship becomes the living presence of Christ and are His messengers of love, compassion, and grace.

About the Author

Duane Eastman lives in Anacortes, Washington with his wife Myrna. Most of the churches he served were wounded, either from congregational conflict or pastoral dysfunction. With an emphasis on grace and love as the keys to personal and congregational renewal, healthy churches became the mark of his pastoral experience and is the source for this book.

Printed in the United States
By Bookmasters